Plants
Taste
Better

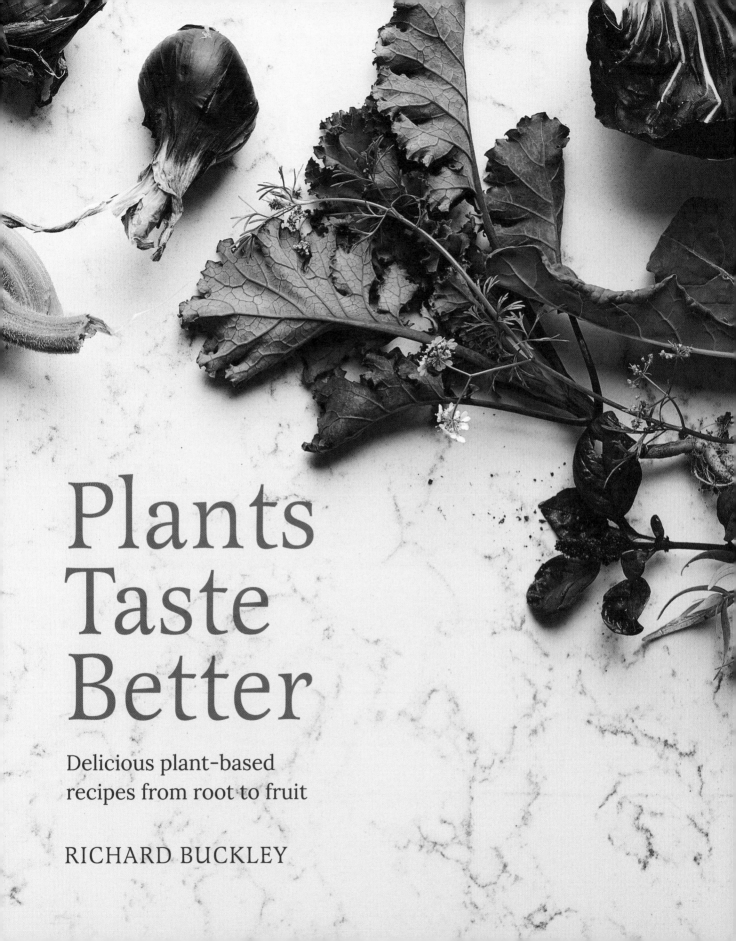

Plants
Taste
Better

Delicious plant-based
recipes from root to fruit

RICHARD BUCKLEY

For Helen, Noah and Otis

Quarto

Design and layout copyright © 2018, 2024
Quarto Publishing Group plc
Photography copyright © Kim Lightbody
Text copyright © Richard Buckley

First published in 2018 by Jacqui Small

This updated edition first published in 2024
by White Lion Publishing, an imprint of
The Quarto Group.
1 Triptych Place
London, SE1 9SH
www.Quarto.com

A catalogue record for this book is available from
the British Library.

ISBN: 978-0-7112-9218-5
eBook ISBN: 978-0-7112-9219-2

Printed in China

MIX
Paper | Supporting
responsible forestry
FSC® C016973

CONTENTS

INTRODUCTION

cooking with plants

We've all cooked plants before, be it boiling a carrot, baking a loaf of bread or brewing a cup of coffee. There is nothing special about it, but it does require care to produce the best results. Plants and fungi are amazing organisms and they make up the majority of the flavours in our diet. Think of any dish – from a curry to the most complex Michelin-starred meal – and I can guarantee that most of the flavours come from plants. I have spent 15 years studying plants as food, how they fit into our culture and how to get the most out of them. Over time I found many wonderful techniques and realized that I was producing the best flavours when I focused on the plants, not on the animals, or lack of.

This book is not a manual, it is a series of practical examples for cooking plants carefully and with skill at home, taking into consideration the raw ingredient itself, the craft traditions that surround it and the culinary principles of fine cookery. It is not necessary to cook every recipe or to cook every part of every plate of food, but I hope the idea that plants can be cooked with grace will permeate through everything you produce and will influence the way that you look at plants from that point onwards.

understanding plants

Take a carrot and hold it in your hand. It's a carrot, right? Yes, but before that it is a root vegetable and before that it is part of a plant. Broadly speaking, all plants are the same. They have roots in the ground, stems to connect and support the various parts, leaves to capture the energy from the sun, flowers to help them reproduce, and fruits and seeds to create more plants the same as themselves. There is infinite variety within this, but the structure remains the same.

When we talk of a vegetable, herb, fruit or seed we are really just talking about a part of a plant that, either through chance or cultivation, we find is well suited to our diet and culinary traditions. We eat plant parts that share similar characteristics. We only eat taproots that swell with sugars and starches to provide energy for the next year. We don't eat the spindly or woody roots of grass or hazel trees. We eat the leaves that are large and mild in flavour as salads, and those that are small and strongly flavoured as herbs. The seeds surrounded by fruits we call nuts, and those that come from pods we call beans. Those that are small and intense in flavour we call spices, and those that are high in starches we call grains.

The ingenuity and craft traditions that have emerged and evolved over the centuries in our treatment of plants are for me some of the fascinations and deep pleasures of cookery: from stone-grinding flour to fermenting cabbage, the connection of the cook to the ingredient, and through it the processes of the natural world, are a source of endless wonder. That said, these traditional processes tend to make use of the same characteristics of the plant part they are using and we tend to use the same techniques for each part of the plant. We roast nuts and seeds to release their intense flavours: there is little difference between roasting almonds

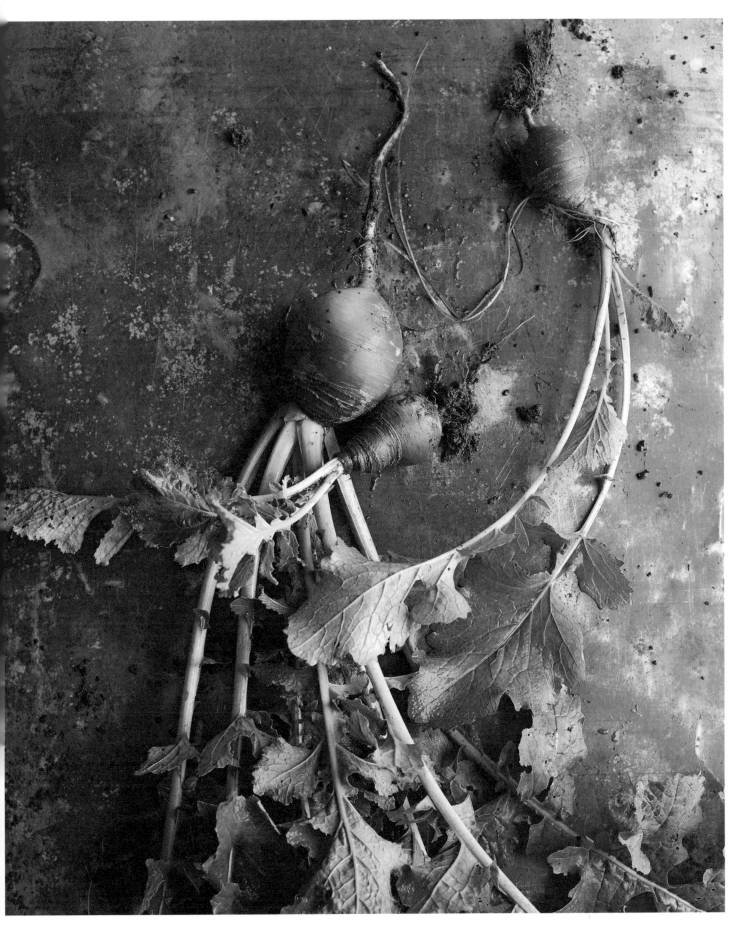

and toasting cumin in terms of what we are trying to achieve and the methods we are using. We cook beans and grains with water to hydrate and modify the starches and make them more digestible; soaking and boiling beans is essentially the same process as combining water with flour and baking it to make bread – you are hydrating and heating. We slice stems across their width to break the chewy fibres that give them strength as a plant and we cook leaves lightly to preserve their delicate colour and structure. An in-depth examination of each plant part and the best cooking techniques for them is well beyond the scope of this book; however, your cooking will improve instantly and for ever if you simply begin to think of the ingredients in front of you as parts of a plant with certain characteristics and the cooking technique merely as a way of enhancing and manipulating those characteristics to suit our appetites and those of our guests.

root to fruit

We waste so many ingredients in the kitchen. People who throw the core from a broccoli or cauliflower in the bin are losing one of the best parts of the vegetable. Carrot tops are lovely and grassy as a herb, and fennel fronds make the best garnish there is. Trying to apply the nose-to-tail philosophy popular in butchery doesn't quite work for plants as parts of some of them are poisonous, such as the leaves of rhubarb or the almond-like stones of apricots. Another issue is that we have developed the varieties of plants we eat over generations of selective breeding so there is very little wild about them. The shoots on the top of a celeriac (celery root) are a celery of sorts, and they are great in a stock, but true celery has been bred to be less woody and stringy. They are the same thing but with a different emphasis. The same can be said of beetroot (beet) tops: they can be cooked but have a much stronger iron flavour than the varieties that are bred for the leaf with a spindly little root at the bottom.

I believe that if a vegetable has multiple edible parts then it is a crime to simply throw a bit away because it is not the part you want. A great many recipes in here follow that philosophy implicitly. My cauliflower hearts dish (see page 174) was designed to use the whole cauliflower head, not because it's trendy but because it's the right thing to do. If you are lucky enough to get your cauliflower surrounded by the leaves you can even use these in place of the kale in the purée. If your beetroot (beets) have leaves on them, keep them and sauté them as an extra garnish. If your fennel in the garden has bolted and gone to seed, wait for the fresh seeds to emerge and harvest them for the freshest, cleanest aniseed flavour you've ever tasted. Sprinkled over a poached pear, they are a revelation.

keep it in the family

Most plants that look the same are from the same family. Almonds, apricots, peaches and cherries all share an ancestor or three. Almonds became as prized for their seed as the others did for their flesh. Some are less obvious – tomatoes, potatoes and aubergines (eggplants) are all members of the nightshade family. Thinking of them in this way can help you to break down the cultural bias you have around a plant and see it in a new light. Courgettes (zucchini) are related to pumpkin, melon and cucumber, and considering them as part of that family breaks them from the ratatouille-shaped box they probably live in. Carrots, fennel, cumin, parsley and celery are all umbellifers, their seeds, roots, flowers and leaves all relate wonderfully to each other and create some really interesting harmonies and substitutions. Rhubarb and buckwheat anyone? Jerusalem artichoke and sunflower seeds? Once you start to think of plants in this way the connections are endless.

THE CRAFT OF PLANT-BASED COOKING

choosing your ingredients

It is almost a cliché but the dishes you make will only taste of what you put in them. The greatest chef in the world cannot make the red balls of foam that appear in supermarkets in the depths of the English winter labelled "tomatoes" taste like anything worth eating.

Organic is better than non-organic, but the label is not important. When you eat a plant you are eating an entire ecosystem, the minerals and flavours in an ingredient come from the land it is grown in and the air that surrounds it. The organic movement has helped to push real farming techniques to the fore, but what really matters is the care of the soil. I would rather buy vegetables from a small grower at a farmers' market who cares for and respects their soil, but cannot afford an organic certification, than I would organic produce from a supermarket that is grown in a big sterile monoculture. Remember organic is focused on what chemicals *aren't* used in growing, not on the positive growing techniques used. Going to your local market allows you to meet the growers and find out how they grow their crops. If they talk about soil more than yield, you know you are on to a winner. You do need to use your own judgement though; just because they are a small producer using organic methods it does not mean they are a skilled grower. The organic movement does attract a number of growers whose enthusiasm for the ethics exceeds their love of the plants. If their produce is poor quality then no amount of good intention is going to make up for it and you are better off in a decent supermarket.

It feels unnecessary to say in this day and age, but it is rarely worth buying plants out of their season. You may be able to buy strawberries and peaches in the winter but there is little point to them, they taste of nothing and often have a strange texture. If you know that something is not at its best then it is best not to buy it.

I have chosen the recipes in this book so that you can find nearly all the ingredients you need in your local supermarket. I would rather focus on the skill and technique of cooking than showing off obscure ingredients no one can find. However, I would encourage you to leave the safety of the aisles if you can and support and meet your local farmers and growers. Your food will taste better and will have whole new layers of meaning as you connect the person who grew the ingredients and the land they did it on to the food on your plate.

flavour and taste

We often use the terms "flavour" and "taste" interchangeably, but they are different things. I think of flavour as the combined experience of the aroma of the food experienced retronasaly, through the back of the nose, and the taste of the food in the mouth. Taste is those experiences that happen within the mouth – the recognized five tastes: salt, sweet, acidic, bitter and umami, as well as the emerging recognition of a fat taste and also astringency (the heat of chilli and mustard).

You need to balance the tastes of a dish making sure the elements are all in check and nothing stands out unless it needs to, as in the acidity of pickles. I always think of taste like the rhythm section of a blues band, you need the drive and groove before you scatter the aromas, the melody, over the top. You can use one taste to balance another; for example, sweetness will balance bitterness, but so will salt. Acidity will balance an overly salty dish and bitterness will add interest to an overly sweet food. This art is complex and my only advice is to trust your instincts and to eat lots of fine food so you can learn instinctively where the "sweet spot" is. People who eat a lot of junk food tend to balance food to taste like junk food, with high salt, sugar and acidity. When matching flavours and aromas, the general rule is "like matches like" – foods that go well together tend to share common aroma compounds.

seasoning with salt

Seasoning is probably the single most important cooking skill you can master, and often the most misunderstood. Salt should not be thought of as a flavour in itself, unless you are putting it on top of breads or crackers. Instead it is generally used as a flavour enhancer, a way of drawing out the flavour of the ingredients in the dish. When a recipe says "season to taste" it does not mean "add salt to your liking", it means "taste the food and add salt until you have achieved the correct flavour balance". Broadly speaking, this amount is objective – there is a correct amount of salt. There may be slight differences in the amount of salt people can biologically taste, but it is a small percentage difference, not the difference between the small pinch my mum adds (who has heard that too much salt is bad for you), and the spoonfuls a young chef may add. When seasoning you are looking for the flavours to come alive, to be bright and vibrant and to feel full in the mouth. As a rule of thumb, if a dish tastes thin and watery, it needs more salt; if you can taste salt, you've added too much. Another tip is to cook your salt in; whenever you add an ingredient to the pan add a small pinch of salt along with it, building up the seasoning as you go. Salt added at the end of cooking will always be more pronounced as a flavour in a dish. It is also important to remember that, when seasoning something hot that will be served cold, you need more seasoning the colder it will be. For example, pâté needs to taste slightly over-seasoned while hot to be correctly seasoned when served cold. It is worth noting that sugar works in the same way; it seasons dishes following the same rules. When we speak of savoury food and desserts we are merely differentiating between foods seasoned with salt or sugar.

In this book I have generally given an accurate weight of salt for each recipe. This is to ensure that those unsure in the craft of seasoning have a clear guide as to how much salt is correct. Those confident with their seasoning can add salt to their own taste, but if the dish doesn't taste as delicious as you think it should, it's probably because you haven't added enough. The quantities given are for Maldon sea salt, a flaked sea salt from the UK. Every salt brings its own character and mineral balance to a dish and Maldon has the distinction of being widely available, very clean and drawing out the top notes in food very well. Feel free to use another flaked sea salt, but be aware that those with a high mineral content, such as fleur de sel, may take less salt before you begin to taste it. If you are adding salt to water for blanching then fine sea salt is adequate and cost-effective when using large quantities.

adding cayenne pepper

I use a lot more cayenne pepper than I do black pepper. This is not to say that black pepper does not have a place, it is a wonderful flavour, but I find cayenne pepper cleaner and more precise. When adding cayenne pepper to a dish you are not looking to add a flavour or even taste the pepper, you are using the pepper to lengthen the flavour of the other ingredients in the mouth. This makes the experience of the item seasoned with cayenne linger longer on the palette and take a more pronounced place in the dish.

umami

Umami is the taste in food that makes you go "Mmm, I'll have some more of that". We call it moreish, depth of flavour, savoury and even "yum". It is very in vogue to talk about umami in plant-based cookery, but you need a little bit of understanding to really get the most from it.

Umami is created by three separate chemicals:

Glutamate: This is found in plant and dairy products. It is most prevalent in fermented foods (it is the "yum factor" in sauerkraut and cheese) and slow-cooked foods such as slow-baked onions. Some of the highest plant-based sources of glutamate are soy sauce, kombu, miso, sauerkraut, sweet potatoes and onions.

Guanylate: This is found in its highest concentrations in mushrooms, especially dried mushrooms. Shiitake, morels and porcinis top the list, while nori is the only non-mushroom or meat ingredient in the top ten.

Inosinate: This is found exclusively in meat products, so is of little use to us here.

Using foods high in any one of these will greatly enhance the yummy savouriness of a food stuff. The real magic happens when you combine two of these elements together in a dish. They enhance the flavour by a degree many, many times that of just one on its own. In the perfect mushroom risotto (see page 147) I have combined massive amounts of guanylate from the dried mushrooms and other mushrooms, with glutamate from the shallots, garlic and mirepoix (see page 63). If you really wanted to give it a kick, you could use some soy sauce in place of the salt, but I am fundamentally against these umami short cuts. If you look at a lot of plant-based recipes they add soy sauce, yeast powder or miso to food stuffs that have no need of these flavours. You can get the umami from plants through solid cooking techniques and taking your time – you don't need to add it where it isn't naturally found. Step away from the soy sauce when making a tomato sauce and figure out how to enhance the depth of flavour naturally by the long, slow cooking of the tomatoes.

texture in food

When we think of a great meal we often think of how it tasted or how it looked, but we rarely think of its texture. Texture is often key to how much we enjoy a dish and, if it is done well, no one even notices. The important thing is to have a variety of textures on the plate and to have them separated so that each mouthful is subtly different: one creamy and smooth, one firm, and one crunchy. This helps to keep us interested when eating a big plate of food. A bowl of risotto tastes great, but a whole bowl of it can be a challenge. However, put some chunky vegetables in and a scattering of crunchy nuts over the top and you can eat the whole thing and still want more.

the colour of food

After flavour and texture, colour is probably my next priority when creating a dish. It is so important that the colours are clean and vibrant. It is also important that a dish with a colour in its name shows that colour clearly. Green lentils are wonderful. They have a hearty, earthy flavour, but, once cooked, they're not green, and if you blend them they go grey. The problem is that you will need to call the dish "green" lentils so people know what it contains, and then people will be expecting green on the plate. I add herbs and spinach to the green lentil & onion pâté (see page 72) to ensure that the green colour is evident, and I choose my flavours wisely to support the plainer, northern European style I am working with. In much the same way I add turmeric or saffron to yellow split peas, so they remain yellow.

equipment

All you need to cook great food is a sharp knife and somewhere to get things hot. You can produce wonderful things with a camping stove and pen knife provided the ingredients are good. That said, this book is full of modern recipes that make liberal use of specialist kitchen equipment. Below is a summary of the items I would consider key in a modern plant-based kitchen, but check the recipe before you begin, to make sure you have everything you need.

Knives

It is not worth buying expensive knives if you cannot sharpen them properly. Whet stones are the gold standard for sharpening knives, and it is worth taking the time to learn how to use one properly – there are many excellent videos available online. As a rule of thumb, you should spend as much money on your sharpening stone as you do on your knife. Good knives take a finer edge and stay sharp for longer, but all knives are the same after a month if you don't sharpen them. You are better off with a discount store knife that you sharpen well and regularly than a hand-made Japanese santoku you have never sharpened.

High-power blender

I use a blender a lot, and nearly every recipe in this book requires one. Buy a good blender with a high-power motor, basically a jet engine with a blade attached. Look for brands that emphasize smoothie making as these tend to have a bit more punch to them. Ones that come with a stick or paddle to stir while blending are often a good bet as well. The better your blender, the smoother and more refined your food will be, it's as simple as that.

Scales

A good set of electronic scales that measure down to 1g is important. Volume measurements such as litres and cups are not accurate enough for really fine cookery. A second set of small scales that weigh down as far as 0.01g are also key for modern ingredients such as xanthan gum and agar. There is no need to buy expensive ones, the most important thing is that they can weigh up to 2.5kg (5½lb) and down to 1g.

Mandolin

There are lots of expensive mandolins on the market, but I like the cheap, plastic Japanese ones as they are easy to use, sharp as a razor and easy to sharpen.

Pestle and mortar

A heavy granite mortar is ideal, but avoid those made of black granite for things like aioli, because they will turn it grey.

Pots and pans

Heavy-based saucepans will make cooking easier by holding a more stable temperature, but as long as it doesn't leak, a skilled cook can use any saucepan to make great food.

Ice-cream maker

If you're going to make a lot of the recipes from the desserts chapter (see page 185) then you will want an ice-cream maker. Those that have a built-in freezing system will produce better textures, but a cheap, pre-freeze model is better than no machine at all.

Dehydrator

This is a luxury, but it means you can be drying things out while using your oven for other purposes. Look for front-loading, tray-style machines rather than the round stacked ones.

SNACKS

These nuts and seeds bring a salty depth of flavour and crunchy texture to any plate of food, or make a simple moreish snack when hunger strikes. Obviously you need to pair them well – a lovely Spanish-inspired salad doesn't sit well with the Eastern-tinged tamari flavours. The main challenge is not eating them all as soon as you make them.

Makes: 1 small jar of each

TAMARI SEEDS

20g (¾oz/⅛ cup) pumpkin seeds
40g (1½oz/⅓ cup) sunflower seeds
10g (¼oz/1¼ tbsp) poppy seeds
10g (¼oz/4 tsp) sesame seeds
1g (½ tsp) coriander seeds
1g (½ tsp) fennel seeds
25ml (1fl oz/5 tsp) tamari (or dark soy sauce such as shoyu)

Preheat the oven to (fan) 160°C/180°C/350°F/gas mark 4. Mix all the seeds together on a baking tray (sheet), spread out evenly and roast for 5 minutes until just golden. Transfer to a bowl, add the tamari and stir to evenly coat.

Return the coated seeds to the baking tray (sheet) and spread them out evenly. Bake for 4 minutes, then stir and spread out again. Bake for a further 4 minutes, then check – you want the tamari to look dry. If it is still wet, then stir and return to the oven in 2-minute bursts until dry.

Move the seeds around the baking tray (sheet) to stop them sticking and then leave until cold and crisp. The seeds will keep in an airtight jar for up to 3 months.

TAMARI CASHEWS

200g (7oz/1½ cups) cashew nuts
80ml (3fl oz/⅓ cup) tamari (or dark soy sauce such as shoyu)

Put the cashew nuts on a baking tray (sheet) then follow the recipe for Tamari Seeds (above). These will keep in an airtight jar for up to 3 months.

FRIED SPANISH ALMONDS

200g (7oz/1½ cups) whole almonds (with skin on)
50ml (2fl oz/scant ¼ cup) extra virgin olive oil
sea salt

Put the almonds into a small heatproof bowl. Pour over boiling water to cover and leave until cool. Drain the almonds and pop them from their skins.

Gently heat the olive oil in a small frying pan (skillet). Add the peeled almonds and fry gently until a light golden brown, stirring and tossing them often. Drain the almonds through a sieve set over a bowl and discard the oil. Transfer the cooked almonds to a bowl lined with kitchen (paper) towel, liberally sprinkle with salt and leave to drain. These will keep in an airtight jar for up to 2 weeks.

These fritters are delicious and nutritious. They are not subtle, however, so I wouldn't serve them with a delicate fine dining meal, but they do make a great snack, light starter or tapas on a summer's day.

Serves: 4

ALMOND & PAPRIKA FRITTERS

FOR THE FILLING

3g (1½ tsp) cumin seeds
6g (⅛oz/2½ tsp) mild smoked
    paprika
2g (generous ½ tsp) agar powder
3g (½ tsp) sea salt
150g (5½oz/1 cup) blanched
    almonds
25ml (1fl oz/5 tsp) extra virgin
    olive oil
150g (5½oz) diced onions
4 cloves of garlic, puréed
    (see page 145)
200ml (7fl oz/generous ¾ cup)
    water
0.75g (scant ½ tsp) cayenne pepper
7g (¼oz/2 tbsp) parsley leaves,
    chopped
4g (4¾ tsp) chopped tarragon
    leaves

FOR THE BATTER

80g (2¾oz/¾ cup) gram flour,
    plus extra to coat
20g (¾oz/2½ tbsp) cornflour
    (cornstarch)
1g (scant ¼ tsp) sea salt
4g (1¾ tsp) paprika
1g (¼ tsp) baking powder
160ml (5½fl oz/⅔ cup) cold water
vegetable oil, for deep-fat frying

TO SERVE

aioli (see page 36)
tomato chutney (see page 38)

Page 22: *almond & paprika fritters with aioli. Page 23: Spanish fried cauliflower (top) and tempura kale (bottom) with tomato chutney.*

Preheat the oven to (fan) 160°C/180°C/350°F/gas mark 4.

Toast the cumin seeds in a frying pan (skillet) over a medium heat until fragrant, then, using a pestle and mortar, grind to a powder. Add the paprika, agar and salt and set aside. Put the almonds on a baking tray (sheet) and toast in the oven for 7 minutes until golden.

Heat the olive oil in a frying pan (skillet), add the onion and fry until just beginning to soften. Add the garlic and cook until the onions are soft and translucent. Add the cumin and paprika mix to the onions, stir to combine, then add the measured water and bring to the boil.

Remove from the heat and transfer to a food processor. Add the almonds and process to a coarse paste. Fold through the cayenne pepper and chopped herbs and pour the mix into a bowl. Cover the top with cling film (plastic wrap) in contact with the mix to prevent a skin forming and put into the fridge for at least 30 minutes to set.

Make the aioli (see page 36) and tomato chutney (see page 38).

Once the fritter mix is set, take it out of the fridge and stir. Form into balls a little smaller than a ping pong ball and place on a plate.

Make the batter. Sieve all the dry ingredients together into a bowl, add the cold water and whisk to form a batter. Put some extra gram flour in a shallow bowl. Prepare your deep-fat fryer (see below).

Put the shaped fritters first into the dry gram flour to coat them and then, using a fork, dip them into the batter mix and then drop them into the hot oil, cooking a few at a time until they float to the surface and are golden brown. If using a deep-fat fryer, shake the basket so they don't stick. If using a saucepan, use a wooden spoon to prevent them sticking to the bottom. You may need to flip them over, using a spoon, to ensure they are evenly cooked. Once cooked remove and drain on kitchen (paper) towel, then serve hot with aioli and tomato chutney.

PREPARING YOUR DEEP-FAT FRYER

Fill a medium saucepan two-thirds full of a neutral vegetable oil or fill a deep-fat fryer with vegetable oil following the manufacturer's instructions. Heat the oil to 190°C/375°F (or slightly lower if you want a slightly slower cooking time). Place a baking tray (sheet) lined with kitchen (paper) towel next to the fryer and have a slotted spoon to hand.

If you are making the almond & paprika fritters (see opposite), it is worth making the cauliflower fritters at the same time as they go very well together. You can use the fritter batter for the cauliflower if you wish. The tempura kale has a light, crispy batter and is one of the simplest, tastiest ways to cook kale that I know of.

Each serves: 4

CAULIFLOWER FRITTERS

FOR THE CAULIFLOWER
1 large cauliflower, cut into
  large florets
5g (⅛ oz/2½ tsp) cumin seeds
5g (⅛ oz/2¼ tsp) smoked paprika
25g (1oz/3½ tbsp) gram flour
vegetable oil, for deep-fat frying

FOR THE BATTER
100g (3½oz/scant 1 cup) gram flour
75g (2¾oz/½ cup) potato flour
3g (½ tsp) sea salt, finely ground
10g (¼oz/4½ tsp) paprika
350ml (12fl oz/1½ cups) cold water

TO SERVE
aioli (see page 36)
tomato chutney (see page 38)

Bring a large saucepan with 4 litres (7 pints/16 cups) of water and 60g (2oz/scant ¼ cup) of salt to the boil, then add the cauliflower florets. Cook for 3–4 minutes until soft but still al dente then shock in ice-cold water (see page 183). Dry the cauliflower florets, then put into a large bowl. Make the aioli (see page 36) and tomato chutney (see page 38).

Prepare the batter. Sieve the dry ingredients together into a bowl, then add the cold water and whisk to form a batter. Prepare your deep-fat fryer (see opposite).

Grind the cumin seeds to a powder using a pestle and mortar. Add the smoked paprika and gram flour and mix together. Sprinkle over the cauliflower and gently mix so the florets are all covered.

Put the cauliflower into the batter mix and then drop it into the hot oil. If using a deep-fat fryer, shake the basket so the cauliflower doesn't stick. If using a saucepan, use a wooden spoon to prevent it sticking to the bottom. Cook for 2–3 minutes until golden, then drain on kitchen (paper) towel. Repeat with all the cauliflower florets and serve with some fiery aioli.

TEMPURA KALE

FOR THE TEMPURA KALE
20 small, tender kale leaves
300g (10½oz/scant 2½ cups) plain
  (all-purpose) flour
20g (¾oz/2½ tbsp) cornflour
  (cornstarch)
2g (⅓ tsp) sea salt
5g (⅛oz/1 tsp) baking powder
300ml (10fl oz/1¼ cups) cold water
vegetable oil, for deep-fat frying

TO SERVE
aioli (see page 36)

Make the aioli (see page 36). Wash the kale leaves and dry thoroughly.

Make the tempura batter by sieving together 200g (7oz/1⅔ cups) of the flour with the cornflour (cornstarch), salt and baking powder. Add the cold water and stir loosely to combine with a fork, but do not overstir or your batter will be tough. Prepare your deep-fat fryer (see opposite).

Toss a kale leaf in the remaining flour, dip it into the tempura batter and drop it into the deep-fat fryer. If using a deep-fat fryer, shake the basket so the kale doesn't stick. If using a saucepan, use a wooden spoon to prevent it sticking to the bottom. Once the batter is golden, remove and drain on kitchen (paper) towel. Repeat for all the kale leaves, cooking them one at a time, and serve with aioli.

| CRISPS |

SWEET POTATO CRISPS

This is a great way to make crisps to add a bit of crunch to a plate. It takes some practice, but it carries more vegetable flavour than deep-frying and keeps a better shape.

Makes: 8 crisps

1 large sweet potato, peeled and cut in half lengthways
1g (scant ¼ tsp) sea salt
4g (1 tsp) caster (superfine) sugar

Preheat the oven to (fan) 140°C/160°C/310°F/gas mark 2½.

Slice the sweet potato finely using a mandolin. Choose 8 of the best slices and place in a bowl. Sprinkle with the salt and sugar and leave for 20 minutes to soften.

Pat the sweet potato slices dry with kitchen (paper) towel and spread them out on a large baking tray (sheet) lined with non-stick baking parchment. Cover with another sheet of baking parchment, pressing down with another slightly smaller tray to make sure the crisps are flat.

Bake the crisps for 7 minutes, then check. If they are starting to crisp, remove the extra baking tray (sheet) and return to the oven for 4-minute bursts until crisp but not coloured. Remove the top sheet of baking parchment and, if needed, return to the oven for 2 minutes maximum to dry out.

Allow the crisps to cool – they should become crispier and brittle as they cool. If they are still a bit wet return them to the oven in short bursts until ready.

These will keep for up to 3 days in an airtight container.

SPRING GREEN CRISPS

A quick, easy-to-make crisp that adds drama, texture and nuttiness to any plate.

Makes: 8–10 crisps

4 large, dark, spring green leaves
extra virgin olive oil, to drizzle
sea salt, to sprinkle

Preheat the oven to (fan) 140°C/160°C/310°F/gas mark 2½.

Trim the spring green leaves, remove and discard the stalk, then cut the leaves into shards approximately 10 x 4cm (4 x 1½ inches). Put the leaves in a small bowl and toss them in a little oil and salt, then spread flat on a large baking tray (sheet) so they are not touching each other.

Bake for 7 minutes, then check. They should look crisp and dry around the edges with no soggy patches, but not burnt on the edges. If they have not reached this point then return them to the oven in 3-minute bursts until ready. Remove from the oven and allow them to cool and go crisp.

These will keep for up to 3 days in an airtight container.

CAVOLO NERO CRISPS

A simple variation of the spring green crisps (see above), but, as cavolo nero is a thicker leaf, you just need to pay a little more attention to check that it has dried fully and isn't still soggy in places.

Makes: 8 crisps

8 cavolo nero leaves
extra virgin olive oil, to drizzle
sea salt, to sprinkle

Preheat the oven to (fan) 160°C/180°C/350°F/gas mark 4. If using large cavolo nero leaves, remove the stem from each leaf and trim the edges if necessary. Toss in a little oil and salt and lay on a baking tray (sheet). Bake in the oven for 10–15 minutes until dry and crisp but not coloured, then leave to cool and crisp up.

These will keep in an airtight container for 3 days.

Hummus is that great vegetarian classic that has become synonymous with plant-based eating, sadly often in a derogatory way. One reason is there are so many recipes that are grainy, bland and uninspiring. Correctly made, hummus is decadent, moreish and elegant. For me, the perfect hummus has a creamy, smooth texture that disappears in the mouth. The trick to achieving this is by peeling the chickpeas (garbanzo beans) and adding enough oil. It may seem like a pain, but peeling your chickpeas (garbanzo beans) will make the difference between a melting, creamy texture and something that is just okay.

Serves: 4

PERFECT HUMMUS

80–100g (2¾–3½oz) dried chickpeas (garbanzo beans) or 400g (14oz) canned (240g/8½oz drained weight)
2g (½ tsp) bicarbonate of soda (baking soda) (if using dried beans)
2g (1 tsp) cumin seeds
2 cloves of garlic, peeled but whole
25ml (1fl oz/5 tsp) lemon juice
40g (1½oz/scant 3 tbsp) tahini
100ml (3½fl oz/scant ½ cup) extra virgin olive oil, plus extra to drizzle
70ml (2½fl oz/generous ¼ cup) cold water
4g (¾ tsp) sea salt

TO SERVE
harissa dressing (see page 39)
zaalouk (see opposite)
flat breads (see page 213)

If using dried chickpeas (garbanzo beans), put them in a bowl and cover with cold water by at least 4cm (1½ inches). Leave for at least 8 hours or ideally overnight.

Make the harissa dressing (see page 39), zaalouk (see opposite) and flat breads (see page 213).

Drain and rinse the dried chickpeas (garbanzo beans) and place in a small lidded saucepan with 1 litre (1¾ pints/4 cups) of cold water and the bicarbonate of soda (baking soda). Bring to the boil and simmer gently for 40–50 minutes, adding more water if it begins to run dry, until the chickpeas (garbanzo beans) are very soft with no grainy texture. When cooked, drain and rinse the chickpeas (garbanzo beans) and put them into a large bowl. Or drain and rinse the canned chickpeas (garbanzo beans), reserving the liquid for aquafaba (see page 36). Rub the chickpeas (garbanzo beans) vigorously between the palms of your hands until the skins come loose (don't worry if they break up a bit). Cover with cold water and agitate them until all the skins float to the surface, removing them as you go. Drain and discard the water and put the peeled chickpeas (garbanzo beans) into a blender.

Put the cumin seeds into a small frying pan (skillet) and heat gently until fragrant but not burnt. Grind to a fine powder using a pestle and mortar and add to the chickpeas (garbanzo beans) along with the rest of the ingredients. Blend for up to 5 minutes, until completely smooth, adding a little more water if necessary. Check the seasoning (see page 13), add more salt if needed, then chill in the fridge for at least 2 hours.

Swirl the hummus into a bowl, add a generous drizzle of olive oil and top with the harissa dressing. Serve with flat breads and zaalouk.

DRIED VERSUS CANNED BEANS

There is always the debate when making something from legumes as to whether it is better to use dried or canned. The feeling is that soaking and cooking dried beans is "proper cooking", and canned beans are a bit of a cheat. There is some truth in this, and it does give you more control over the cooking process; however, dried beans are a seasonal product and should be young and fresh, preferably less than a year old. Old beans have a floury texture, take hours to cook and have no flavour beside that of dried beans. If you can find out how old the beans are, use dried, but if you can't, use the best-quality canned or jarred beans that you can get.

This recipe is a relatively new discovery for me. Until I found this traditional Moroccan recipe the short English aubergine (eggplant) season meant I made babaganoush, which, while delicious, is tainted by hemp shirts and sandals. I think that zaalouk is much more delicious than babaganoush, and it also makes great use of the tomatoes that are ripe at exactly the same time. It always tastes better after a night in the fridge so, if you have time, try to make it at least a day ahead of eating.

Serves: 4

ZAALOUK

1 large aubergine (eggplant) (about 500g/1lb 2oz)
7g (¼oz/3½ tsp) cumin seeds
7g (¼oz/1¼ tsp) sea salt
7g (¼oz/1 tbsp) smoked paprika
4 large plum tomatoes
4 cloves of garlic, puréed (see page 145)
15g (½oz/¼ cup) parsley leaves, finely chopped, plus extra to garnish
30ml (1fl oz/2 tbsp) extra virgin olive oil
75ml (2¾fl oz/⅓ cup) water
10ml (2 tsp) lemon juice
2g (1 tsp) ground black pepper

TO SERVE
harissa dressing (see page 39)
perfect hummus (see opposite)
flat breads (see page 213)
extra virgin olive oil, to drizzle
black pepper

Preheat the oven to (fan) 160°C/180°C/350°F/gas mark 4.

Spike the aubergine (eggplant) with a fork or sharp knife 2 or 3 times and place on a small baking tray (sheet). Roast in the oven for 30 minutes until soft, then leave to cool before cutting in half lengthways. Scoop out the flesh and discard the skin. Cut the flesh into rough dice, each about 1.5cm (½ inch), and transfer to a large frying pan (skillet).

Put the cumin seeds into a small frying pan (skillet) and toast over a medium heat until you can just begin to smell them. Transfer to a pestle and mortar and grind to a powder. Add the salt and smoked paprika, stir, then add to the aubergine (eggplant).

Remove the stem from the tomatoes and cut into 1.5cm (½-inch) dice. Add the tomatoes, garlic, parsley, olive oil and water to the frying pan (skillet) containing the aubergine (eggplant) and bring to a gentle simmer. Cook gently for 30 minutes, stirring often, adding an occasional splash of water if necessary. When ready, the mix should be thick and rich. Add the lemon juice and black pepper and stir to combine.

Transfer to a container, leave to cool, then place in the fridge for at least a few hours and ideally overnight.

Make the harissa dressing (see page 39), perfect hummus (see opposite) and flat breads (see page 213).

When ready to eat, transfer the zaalouk to a serving bowl and add a drizzle of olive oil and a twist of black pepper. Serve with harissa dressing, hummus and flat breads.

I'm a big fan of gram flour: it has a great flavour, is gluten-free and highly nutritious. The trick is to remember to make your batter ahead of time to allow it to ferment overnight. This removes any raw bean flavour and adds a sour nuttiness that is unique to gram flour. You can make this with or without the garlic – it will still work really well without it.

Serves: 4–8

GARLIC PANISSE

250g (9oz/2¼ cups) gram flour
50g (1¾oz/scant ⅓ cup) polenta
   (cornmeal)
1 litre (1¾ pints/4 cups) water
12 cloves of garlic
200ml (7fl oz/generous ¾ cup)
   extra virgin olive oil
8g (¼ oz/1½ tsp) sea salt
vegetable oil, for deep-fat frying

TO SERVE
tomato chutney (see page 38)

You need to make the panisse batter a day in advance. In a bowl, whisk the gram flour, polenta and water together. Leave in a warm place (22°C/71°F) for 24 hours.

Preheat the oven to (fan) 100°C/120°C/240°F/gas mark ¼–½. Place the garlic cloves in a small ovenproof dish and cover completely with the olive oil. Bake in the oven for 30–40 minutes until very soft but not coloured, then allow to cool. (The garlic and oil will keep in the fridge for 3 months.) Make the tomato chutney (see page 38).

Remove the garlic from the oil and grind to a fine paste using a pestle and mortar. Put the panisse batter into a saucepan and add the salt and garlic paste. Whisk to make sure it is smooth, then gently heat, stirring all the time using a silicon spatula. As it approaches the boil it will thicken dramatically – keep stirring until the spatula stands up in the mix.

Pour the mix onto a board or tray lined with non-stick baking parchment. Spread to a 1.5cm (½-inch) thickness. Lay another sheet of baking parchment on top and press down slightly. Leave to cool to room temperature, then transfer to the fridge and chill for 1 hour.

Prepare your deep-fat fryer (see page 24). Cut the chilled panisse into 1.5cm (½-inch) strips, then cut these strips into chips about 3–5cm (1¼–2 inches) long. Deep-fry the panisse in batches for about 2 minutes, then drain on kitchen (paper) towel. Serve hot with tomato chutney.

These polenta chips are a delicious alternative to potato chips and have a fantastic crunchy outer and creamy inner. The rosemary adds a nice herbal note but can be switched for other savoury herbs or even green olives.

The rosti are so simple and delicious it seems a shame to mess with them, but you can add herbs, especially sage or thyme should you wish. Serve either the rosti or polenta chips as part of a plant-based fried breakfast and you will have friends for life.

Each serves: 4

ROSEMARY POLENTA CHIPS

1.1 litres (2 pints/4½ cups) basic stock (see page 62)
225g (8oz/1⅓ cups) polenta (cornmeal), plus extra to dust
5g (⅛oz/3 tbsp) rosemary, finely chopped
40ml (1½fl oz/8 tsp) extra virgin olive oil
5g (⅛oz/1 tsp) sea salt
vegetable oil, for deep-fat frying

TO SERVE
aioli (see page 36)
tomato chutney (see page 38)

Make the aioli (see page 36) and tomato chutney (see page 38).

Put the stock into a saucepan and bring to the boil. Sprinkle in the polenta (cornmeal), whisk with a wire whisk until it begins to thicken, then stir continuously with a wooden spoon or silicon spatula. When it is thick enough that the wooden spoon stands up in it, add the rosemary, olive oil and salt and stir well to combine.

Pour onto a large board lined with non-stick baking parchment and spread out into a rectangle 1cm (½ inch) thick. Allow to cool completely, then cut into 1cm (½-inch) strips. Cut these into chip shapes and dust with polenta (cornmeal). Prepare your deep-fat fryer (see page 24).

Deep-fry (see page 24) or shallow-fry the chips in batches (they will take 2–4 minutes), then drain on kitchen (paper) towel. Serve hot with tomato chutney and aioli.

ROSTI

900g (2lb) floury potatoes, such as rooster or maris piper
100g (3½oz) finely sliced onions
10g (¼oz/1¾ tsp) sea salt
30g (1¼oz/4 tbsp) gram flour
rapeseed oil, to fry

TO SERVE
aioli (see page 36)
tomato chutney (see page 38)

Wash but don't peel the potatoes, then coarsely grate into a large bowl and add the onion and salt. Massage with your fingers, then transfer to a colander over a large bowl and leave to drain for 1 hour, occasionally pressing the mix down and mixing it around.

Make the aioli (see page 36) and tomato chutney (see page 38).

After 1 hour remove the potato mix and squeeze to remove as much liquid as possible. Transfer the mix to a clean bowl and loosen with your fingers. Sieve the gram flour over and mix with your fingers so the potato is evenly covered.

Preheat the oven to its lowest setting. Take 1 tablespoon of the mix and form into a flat fritter shape about 7mm (⅓ inch) thick. Lay out on a tray and repeat with the rest of the mix. Cover the base of a large frying pan (skillet) with about 5mm (¼ inch) of rapeseed oil and heat to 180°C/350°F. Add the rosti in batches and fry until golden and crisp on one side, then turn over. Fry until golden on the other side, then place on a lined baking tray (sheet) and keep warm in the oven while you cook the rest, topping up with more oil if necessary. Serve hot with tomato chutney and aioli.

| ACCOMPANIMENTS |

AIOLI

True aioli is a thing of beauty, incredibly garlicky and very hard to make. This version is technically a garlic mayonnaise but is foolproof to make and I think tastes more palatable than its fearsome namesake. Use the oil you prefer, bearing in mind that olive oil will be very strongly flavoured.

Makes: 300ml (10fl oz) jar

50ml (2fl oz/scant ¼ cup) aquafaba (see below)
1–2 cloves of garlic
20ml (¾fl oz/4 tsp) cider vinegar or 25ml (1fl oz/5 tsp) lemon juice
2g (⅓ tsp) sea salt
150ml (5fl oz/⅔ cup) oil (see above)

Put the aquafaba, garlic, cider vinegar (or lemon juice) and salt into a blender and blend until smooth. Transfer the oil to a jug or container you can pour slowly from.

Set your blender onto a medium speed and very slowly add the oil, a small splash at a time until about half of it has gone into creating a smooth, glossy, emulsified liquid. Speed up the pouring and as you near the end the mix will miraculously turn into a thick glossy mayonnaise and you will be unable to blend any more. This will keep in a jar in the fridge for up to a month.

AQUAFABA

I refused to even try aquafaba for a long time, treating it as I do all substitutes, with barely concealed contempt. Aquafaba is the water left after you have cooked legumes. The proteins from the legumes transfer to the cooking water and behave exactly like the proteins in egg whites, forming stable foams and meringues and can be used in exactly the same quantities. When first experimenting simply open a can of chickpeas (garbanzo beans) and use the water from this, ensuring it is not salted. As you get more confident you can make your own. Simply soak 400g (14oz) of beans or chickpeas (garbanzo beans) overnight in cold water and refresh. Put in a lidded saucepan with 1.8 litres (3¼ pints/7½ cups) of water and simmer for about 60 minutes until cooked. Allow to cool in the water, then strain out the beans and the remaining water is aquafaba. You can reduce it further to make it even stronger, but its beany flavour will be more pronounced.

BLACK OLIVE TAPENADE

I use this as a salty foil for the sweet tomatoes in the confit tomato salad (see page 104), but it is a great thing to have to hand and eat with bread and wine when the mood takes you. For an extra-special version use half extra virgin olive oil and half black truffle oil.

Makes: 250ml (8½fl oz) jar

200g (7oz/1¼ cups) pitted kalamata olives, rinsed and drained
20g (¾oz/⅛ cup) capers, rinsed and drained
15ml (1 tbsp) red wine vinegar
50ml (2fl oz/scant ¼ cup) extra virgin olive oil (or see above)

Put all the ingredients into a food processor and process to make a paste. This will keep in the fridge for at least 2 weeks.

FIG CHUTNEY

Just typing this recipe is making my mouth water. This is my favourite chutney in the world and is a great way to add sweet and sour depth to any salad or lunch.

Makes: 500ml (18fl oz) jar

250g (9oz/1⅔ cups) dried figs
1 onion, diced
1 Bramley apple, peeled, cored and diced
20g (¾oz) organic ginger (see page 58), grated
finely grated zest of 1 lemon
125ml (4fl oz/½ cup) cider vinegar
100g (3½oz/generous ½ cup) soft brown sugar
5g (⅛ oz/2½ tsp) mild Madras curry powder
1g (⅔ tsp) chilli flakes (crushed chilli)
4g (¾ tsp) sea salt
300ml (10fl oz/1¼ cups) water

Remove and discard the stalks from the figs and cut each fig into 8 pieces. Put all the ingredients into a small saucepan and simmer gently for up to an hour until everything has completely broken down. Leave to cool, then store in a sealed jar or container. This will keep in a jar in the fridge for at least 3 months.

« mustard

« fig chutney

« aioli

tomato chutney »

pesto »

TOMATO CHUTNEY

Some recipes, like the garlic panisse (see page 34), or rosemary polenta chips (see page 35), while delicious on their own, are really just vehicles for a good sauce or chutney. If that is the case then this is the chutney you need. It's not clever, but it is very, very tasty. Make a lot as it will keep for ages in the fridge, and you can eat it with anything that comes out of your deep-fat fryer.

Makes: 500ml (18fl oz) jar

3g (1½ tsp) cumin seeds
5g (⅛ oz/2 tsp) smoked paprika
5g (⅛ oz/1 tsp) sea salt
25ml (1fl oz/5 tsp) extra virgin olive oil
1 banana shallot, finely diced
1 red chilli, halved, deseeded, finely chopped
10g (¼oz) organic ginger (see page 58), finely grated
1 clove of garlic, puréed (see page 145)
3g (1½ tsp) fennel seeds
400g (14oz) can of plum tomatoes
150g (5½oz/generous ¾ cup) soft brown sugar
75ml (2¾fl oz/⅓ cup) red wine vinegar

Fry the cumin seeds in a small frying pan (skillet) until fragrant, then grind to a fine powder using a pestle and mortar. Add the smoked paprika and salt and mix.

Gently heat the olive oil in a saucepan. Add the shallot and cook for 1 minute, then add the chilli, ginger and garlic and fry briefly. Add the fennel seeds and paprika/cumin mix and then add the tomatoes. Cook until the tomatoes are broken down and thick, then add the sugar and vinegar. Cook until thick and glossy. Remove from the heat and leave to cool.

This will keep in a jar in the fridge for up to 3 months.

PESTO

As with most things made with raw garlic, this will taste better if left to mellow overnight. Use the best-quality basil you can find – this is a basil sauce after all!

Makes: 500ml (18fl oz) jar

100g (3½oz/¾ cup) pine nuts
2 cloves of garlic, chopped
2g (⅓ tsp) sea salt
150g (5½oz/6 cups) basil leaves, roughly chopped
250ml (8½fl oz/1 cup) extra virgin olive oil
50ml (2fl oz/scant ¼ cup) lemon juice

Preheat the oven to (fan) 160°C/180°C/350°F/gas mark 4. Put the pine nuts onto a small baking tray (sheet) and roast in the oven for 7 minutes until just golden brown. Set aside to cool.

If making by hand, grind the garlic and salt to a paste using a large pestle and mortar. Add the pine nuts and smash to a coarse crumb. Add the basil a little at a time, grinding it to a paste before adding the next batch. If it starts to get too thick, add a little oil to loosen. Once all the basil is incorporated, add any remaining oil and the lemon juice.

If making in a food processor, process the garlic, salt and pine nuts to a coarse lumpy crumb. Add the basil, oil and lemon juice and process to a coarse purée.

Taste and adjust the seasoning as necessary (see page 13). This will keep in a jar in the fridge for up to a month.

HARISSA

This recipe is based on the Tunisian tradition, hence the generous use of caraway, and I doubt I'll ever look for another harissa recipe now. Which chillies you choose to use is personal: I feel this combination gives good colour and moderate heat but substitute as you prefer. If you use fresh chillies you obviously don't need to soak them, and you can reduce the weight by half. It makes a thick paste which will store for up to 3 months in the fridge, but which isn't very 'saucy'. To use as a sauce, put a little in a bowl and add a splash of water to get the desired consistency.

Makes: 500ml (18fl oz) jar

80g (3oz) dried Kashmiri chillies
80g (3oz) dried De Arbol chillies
100g (3½oz) caraway seeds
100g (3½oz) peeled garlic cloves
20g (¾oz/3½ tsp) sea salt flakes
60ml (2¼fl oz/¼ cup) olive oil

Put the chillies in a heatproof bowl, cover with boiling water and leave to soak for at least 1 hour.

Strain and pat dry the chillies and pull off the stalks. Chop to a coarse paste on a board (the skins won't grind in a mortar).

Toast the caraway seeds lightly then grind in a pestle and mortar. Add the garlic with the salt and grind to a paste. Add the chopped chillies and grind with a little of the oil until combined, to make a paste.

Store in the fridge topped with a little oil until needed.

CARAWAY MUSTARD

This is great simple mustard to have on hand. The caraway mellows over time but always adds a lovely complexity to whatever you are making.

Makes: 500ml (18fl oz) jar

200g (7oz) yellow mustard seeds
30g (1¼oz) caraway seeds
60g (2oz) brown mustard seeds
250g (8¾oz) raw cider vinegar
150ml (5fl oz/⅔ cup) water
15g (½oz) salt

Blend the yellow mustard seeds and caraway seeds together in a blender or spice grinder to a coarse flour consistency. Mix with the rest of the ingredients in a sterile storage container and allow to sit at room temperature for 24 hours.

This mustard is best used after 2 weeks as the bitterness will abate over that time. Store it in the fridge for as long as you need to.

SOUPS, PÂTÉS & LIGHT LUNCHES

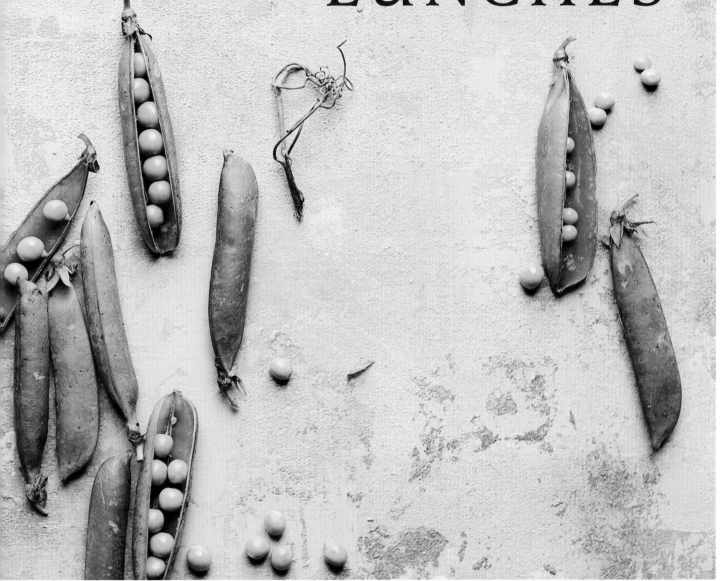

I live in a cottage in rural Somerset and my beautiful little garden is a never-ending source of inspiration through the balmy summer months. Looking out through the kitchen window I can see a profusion of herbs, peas and beans all clambering for space, climbing the walls and tumbling out of pots. This is an attempt to capture that feeling of verdant abundance in a little bowl of chilled soup. The combination I've used is simply what I can lay my hands on straight from the garden, so mix and match depending on what you have available and what is best in season.

Serves: 4

PEA AND HERB SOUP
with almond foam

FOR THE SOUP
25g (1oz/scant 1 cup) spinach
25g (1oz/½ cup) chives
25g (1oz/⅓ cup) parsley
2g (2 tsp) chopped tarragon
250g (9oz/1⅔ cups) freshly podded
    peas
50ml (2fl oz/scant ¼ cup) extra
    virgin olive oil
100g (3½oz) banana shallots, sliced
2.5g (1 tbsp) thyme leaves
350ml (12fl oz/1½ cups) water
sea salt

FOR THE FOAM
50g (1¾oz/⅓ cup) whole almonds
5ml (1 tsp) white wine vinegar
1 clove of garlic
200ml (7oz/generous ¾ cup) water
2g (⅓ tsp) sea salt
soy lecithin

FOR THE GARNISH
100g (3½oz) broad beans (fava
    beans), podded
50g (1¾oz) sugar snap peas,
    deveined
50g (1¾oz/⅓ cup) freshly podded
    peas
1 spring onion (scallion), finely sliced
4 parsley or micro parsley leaves,
    plus extra to top
8 lemon balm leaves
extra virgin olive oil, to drizzle
4 large radishes

First make the soup. Blanch the spinach, chives, parsley and tarragon together until the parsley is wilted and a vibrant green, then shock in ice-cold water (see page 183). Squeeze out the water using your hands, making a ball. Roughly chop and set aside. Refill the saucepan and bring to the boil. Boil the peas for a few minutes until cooked with no grainy texture, then drain and shock in ice-cold water (see page 183).

Heat the olive oil in a saucepan and add the shallots. Cook until soft and translucent, then add the thyme. Cook for 1 minute, leave to cool completely, then transfer to a blender. Add the chopped herbs, peas and measured water. Blend until very smooth, pass through a sieve and season with salt to taste (see page 13). Place in the fridge.

Next make the almond foam. Preheat the oven to (fan) 160°C/180°C/350°F/gas mark 4. Put the almonds onto a small baking tray (sheet) and roast for 10 minutes, until a dark colour. Transfer to a blender, add the vinegar, garlic, water and salt and blend until very smooth.

Line a sieve with a 30cm (12-inch) square muslin (cheesecloth) and set it over a jug. Pour the almond mix into the sieve and collect up the corners to make a bag. Twist the bag to squeeze out as much liquid as you can. Discard the almond meal in the bag and then measure the liquid. For every 100ml (3½fl oz/scant ½ cup) of liquid add 1.5g (⅔ tsp) of soy lecithin. Using a stick blender, blend the lecithin into the mix.

Next make the garnish. Blanch the broad beans (fava beans), sugar snap peas and podded peas until just soft, then shock in ice-cold water (see page 183). Dry on kitchen (paper) towel then place in a bowl, reserving a few sugar snap pea pods for garnish, add the spring onion (scallion) and shred the parsley and lemon balm over. Drizzle with a little olive oil. Place a pile of the bean and pea mix into each of 4 wide soup bowls. Finely slice the radish on a mandolin to give wafer thin slices and add to the pile along with a couple of just opened sugar snap pea pods.

Using a stick blender, whizz the almond foam at high speed, just skimming the surface of the liquid – keep whizzing until you have a beautiful, dense foam. Spoon the foam next to the pea salad and top with a few sprigs of herbs. Add the soup or pour the soup at the table from a jug for added effect.

This is a very simple soup but is brought to life by the fermented wadi and fenugreek oil. It tastes purely of cauliflower, and while that is very nice, it is designed as a backdrop for other flavours to play over and not to be eaten all on its own. Feel free to adapt this as you wish, just make sure you give it an interesting garnish and note that if using fenugreek oil, it needs to be made two weeks before using.

Serves: 4

CAULIFLOWER SOUP
with red lentil wadi

FOR THE WADI
200g (7oz/1 cup) red lentils
pinch of asafoetida
1g (¼ tsp) fenugreek powder
pinch of cayenne pepper
3g (½ tsp) sea salt
rapeseed oil, for deep-fat frying

FOR THE SOUP
1.5 litres (2½ pints/6 cups) basic stock (see page 62)
1kg (2¼lb) cauliflower (without the stem or leaves)
40ml (1½fl oz/8 tsp) rapeseed oil
1 onion, sliced
sea salt
2 cloves of garlic, puréed (see page 145)
50ml (2fl oz/scant ¼ cup) extra virgin olive oil or hazelnut oil
pinch of cayenne pepper
fenugreek oil (see page 220) or truffle oil

Make the fenugreek oil (see page 220) at least 2 weeks before using or use truffle oil. You need to start making the red lentil wadi a day before eating. Put the lentils in a bowl and cover with cold water by at least 2cm (¾ inch). Leave to soak for at least 6 hours or preferably overnight.

Drain the lentils and rinse well. Put into a blender with the asafoetida, fenugreek powder and cayenne pepper, and blend until a smooth paste, adding a little water if needed. The mix should be thick enough to stand on a spoon, not runny. Transfer to a sterile container (see page 99) and put in a warm place (22°C/71°F) for 8–24 hours. It should have fermented and taken on a slightly sour aroma. Mix well, stir in the salt, then place in the fridge to firm up.

Next make the soup. Make the basic stock (see page 62). Cut the cauliflower into quarters, then slice each quarter into 1cm (½-inch) slices. Put the rapeseed oil into a large saucepan and heat gently. Add the onion and a generous pinch of salt, turn down the heat and cook gently for about 20 minutes until soft but not coloured. Add the garlic and cook for 3 more minutes, then add the cauliflower and another pinch of salt and cook for 2 minutes. Add the stock, bring to the boil, then simmer gently with a lid on for about 20 minutes until the cauliflower is cooked.

Transfer the cauliflower mix to a blender and add the olive oil. Blend, in batches if necessary, until silky smooth. Pass through a sieve and season with salt and a pinch of cayenne pepper (see page 13). Return to the saucepan and keep warm.

Prepare your deep-fat fryer (see page 24). Take two-thirds of a tablespoon of the wadi mix, and, using another spoon, push it off into the hot oil. Shake the basket to prevent it sticking and add another spoonful. Once they have floated to the surface and are a golden brown colour, flip them over to make sure both sides cook evenly. Remove and drain on kitchen (paper) towel. Continue until all the mix is used.

Serve the wadi floating on top of the cauliflower soup with a drizzle of fenugreek oil over the top.

Sweetcorn is a surprisingly versatile ingredient – lightly boiled it has a sweet simplicity, but charred it is complex and delicious. Bring these two flavour profiles together and you have a balanced plate of food. Although a different variety, popcorn is another delicious way to cook corn. It is simply three nice ways of using the corn in one dish. Adding a touch of madras curry powder helps add some wonderful aromas over the sweet, charred base flavour.

Serves: 4

SWEETCORN SOUP
with charred sweetcorn and curried popcorn

FOR THE SOUP
1 litre (1¾ pints/4 cups) basic stock (see page 62)
25ml (1fl oz/5 tsp) rapeseed oil, plus extra to drizzle
1 onion, sliced
3 yellow (bell) peppers, deseeded and sliced
500g (1lb 2oz) sweetcorn kernels (fresh or frozen)
sea salt

FOR THE CHARRED SWEETCORN
1 ear of sweetcorn
extra virgin olive oil
sea salt

FOR THE GARNISH
extra virgin olive oil, to drizzle
curried popcorn (see page 115)

Make the curried popcorn (see page 115) and the basic stock (see page 62).

Heat the rapeseed oil in a large saucepan and add the onion. Cook gently until soft and translucent, then add the peppers and cook until soft. Next add the sweetcorn and stock. Cover with a lid and bring to the boil. As soon as the soup boils, check the kernels are cooked, and if soft remove from the heat. Leave the mix to cool, then process in a blender (in batches if necessary) until silky smooth. Pass through a sieve into a clean saucepan and season with salt (see page 13). Warm gently while you cook the charred sweetcorn.

Strip the leaves from the sweetcorn and remove any strings. Heat a heavy saucepan to a very high temperature. Add the sweetcorn and cook until it starts to blacken in spots. Turn slightly and repeat until the whole sweetcorn is well charred. Cut into slices and drizzle with olive oil and a generous pinch of salt.

Serve the hot soup in bowls with a good drizzle of olive oil and a scattering of curried popcorn over the top. Serve 1–2 sweetcorn pieces alongside it.

I was served a variation of this soup by my friend Silvana at the Foodie Bugle and it has stuck with me ever since. It took me over a year to summon up the courage to ask her for the recipe, and it has since become a firm summer favourite. My version omits the passata, which she insists is essential to its authenticity, but I find detracts from the freshness.

This is not a fine soup, it is rustic peasant food, made from the freshest, simplest ingredients, and is best made a day in advance for the flavours to mature. To blend it too smoothly detracts from its character. To garnish it, simply add some diced cucumber, tomato, Romano red pepper and onion and pile it on top with a load of fresh herbs, or add a drizzle of peppery olive oil. Serve it cold with crusty bread, and a fresh green salad if you wish.

Serves: 4

GAZPACHO

1 small cucumber, peeled and
   sliced
3 spring onions (scallions), coarsely
   chopped
1 red (bell) pepper, roughly
   chopped
2 cloves of garlic, peeled and
   central stem removed
15g (½oz/⅔ cup) basil
10g (¼oz/generous ⅓ cup)
   oregano
30ml (1fl oz/2 tbsp) extra virgin
   olive oil
45ml (1½fl oz/3 tbsp) red wine
   vinegar
1kg (2¼lb) ripe, juicy tomatoes
   (the best you can find)
sea salt
black pepper

FOR THE GARNISH
½ cucumber, half diced and half
   sliced and rolled
2 tomatoes, diced
1 Romano red pepper, diced
1 small onion or spring onion
   (scallion), sliced
16 small basil leaves
extra virgin olive oil

Put all the gazpacho ingredients, except the tomatoes, salt and pepper, into a blender and process slowly until semi-smooth (this is not meant to be silky smooth). Transfer to a large mixing bowl.

Quarter the tomatoes and add to the blender. Process until almost smooth, with just a bit of texture, then add to the mixing bowl along with salt and pepper to taste (see page 13). Cover and store in the fridge overnight for the flavours to come together.

Serve cold with a garnish of cucumber, tomatoes, Romano red pepper, onion and basil. Add a good glug of olive oil to each bowl and serve.

Leek and potato soup is perhaps the humblest of all meals. Two of the cheapest ingredients you can buy made into a soup, the simplest meal format imaginable. It is also a great test of a cook's skill. Leeks are a difficult vegetable to work with and are most usefully thought of as two vegetables in one. The white part is best treated as an onion, while the green part is better treated as a cabbage. Trying to emphasize the sweet, oniony depth of the leek while keeping the bright green of the top, bringing just enough of the sulphurous edge to add character without ruining the soup, can be tricky. If you don't want to make the leek and potato cakes, then simply serve the soup with a drizzle of your favourite oil.

Serves: 4

LEEK & POTATO SOUP
with leek & potato cakes

FOR THE POTATO CAKES

1 large 400g (14oz) starchy baking potato, washed, but skin left on
sea salt
25ml (1fl oz/5 tsp) extra virgin olive oil
1 leek, finely sliced
7g (¼oz/¾ tbsp) cornflour (cornstarch)
2g (2⅓ tsp) chopped tarragon
sunflower oil, to fry

FOR THE SOUP

800ml (28fl oz/3⅓ cups) basic stock (see page 62)
150g (5½oz) Jersey royal potatoes (or buttery textured new potatoes), washed but not peeled
400g (14oz) tender leeks
1 bay leaf
1 clove
60ml (2¼fl oz/¼ cup) extra virgin olive oil
150g (5½oz) finely sliced onion
sea salt

First make the leek and potato cakes. Chop the potato into 2cm (¾-inch) cubes. Put into a small saucepan, cover with cold water and add ½ teaspoon of salt. Bring to the boil and simmer gently until the potatoes are soft. Heat the olive oil in a small frying pan (skillet) and add the sliced leek. Sweat the leeks until soft and sweet but not coloured.

Drain the potatoes and mash until smooth. Mix in the cornflour (cornstarch), leek and tarragon. Check for seasoning and add salt if needed (see page 13). Spread the mix out onto a work surface and use a 2cm (¾-inch) cookie cutter to cut rounds from the mix, re-flattening and re-cutting when necessary. Set aside.

Next make the soup. Make the basic stock (see page 62). Finely slice the potatoes on a mandolin. Separate the white and green parts of the leeks and finely slice each, keeping them in 2 separate piles. Take a 10cm (4-inch) square piece of muslin (cheesecloth) and place the bay leaf and clove in the middle. Tie diagonally opposite corners together to form a sealed bag.

Heat the olive oil in a saucepan and add the onion and a pinch of salt. Cook until just going soft but not coloured, then add the potatoes and cook for about 4 minutes until just softening. Add the white part of the leeks and fry gently for about 4 minutes, then add the green part of the leeks and fry for 1 minute. Add the stock and muslin (cheesecloth) bag. Bring quickly to the boil and simmer for 5–10 minutes until the potatoes are soft. Remove and discard the muslin (cheesecloth) bag. Transfer the soup to a blender and blend until smooth. Pass the soup through a sieve, adjust the seasoning if necessary (see page 13), and gently reheat while you fry the potato cakes.

Heat a little sunflower oil in a frying pan (skillet) until very hot and then add the potato cakes. Fry until golden brown and then flip over. When crispy and golden on both sides, drain on a plate lined with kitchen (paper) towel. Serve the soup hot (but not boiling) with a drizzle of oil. Add the leek and potato cakes at the end, floating in the soup like croutons.

White onions have a sweeter character and more complex flavour when cooked slowly than the more readily available brown variety. The onions bring sweetness and depth, while the olive oil provides richness and texture. I like to use a mild, buttery olive oil from Provence, as this allows the onions to sing out, but I would avoid the dominating, very peppery Spanish and Italian varieties.

This recipe calls for leek & garlic stock (see page 62). Do not be tempted to substitute this for another stock, it is a key part of the soup's character and is a very quick and easy stock to make.

Because of the slowly stewed onions the soup is quite sweet and the olive oil makes it very rich, so I have added a slightly bitter, salty garnish of roasted black olives and burnt potato to balance the dish. On their own they are too much, but they work magically with this rich, sweet soup.

Serves: 4

WHITE ONION & OLIVE OIL SOUP
with charred new potatoes, beluga lentils and black olives

FOR THE LENTILS
30g (1¼oz/3 tbsp) dried beluga lentils
300ml (10fl oz/1¼ cups) leek & garlic stock (see page 62)
3g (½ tsp) sea salt

FOR THE POTATOES
2 new potatoes
glug of extra virgin olive oil

FOR THE SOUP
4 tsp black olive crumbs (see page 113)
500ml (18fl oz/generous 2 cups) leek & garlic stock (see page 62)
500g (1lb 2oz) sliced white (or brown) onions
50ml (2fl oz/scant ¼ cup) extra virgin olive oil
25ml (1fl oz/5 tsp) top-quality extra virgin olive oil (see introduction, above)
sea salt

Soak the lentils in advance. Put the lentils in a small bowl and cover with cold water by at least 2cm (¾ inch). Place in the fridge to soak for at least 4 hours and ideally overnight. Prepare the black olive crumbs (see page 113) and leek & garlic stock (see page 62) for the lentils and soup.

Preheat the oven to (fan) 160°C/180°C/350°F/gas mark 4. Put the potatoes in a small saucepan with 400ml (13½fl oz/1⅔ cups) of water and 4g (¾ tsp) of salt. Gently bring to the boil and cover with a lid. Simmer gently for 10–20 minutes until soft, then drain.

While the potatoes are boiling, drain and rinse the lentils, then place in a small, lidded saucepan and add the stock and salt. Gently bring to the boil and cook for 15 minutes – they should be soft but hold their shape and colour. If not ready, cook for 5 minutes then check again. Once cooked, drain, discarding the stock, and keep warm.

Meanwhile, make the soup. Place the onions and 50ml (2fl oz/scant ¼ cup) of olive oil in a large saucepan. Gently heat the onions until they begin to fry and then turn down the heat. Cover with a cartouche (see page 182) and stew gently until the onions are soft. Add the stock and bring to the boil. Once boiling, remove from the heat and allow to cool slightly before adding the top-quality olive oil.

Toss the new potatoes in the olive oil, place on a small baking tray (sheet) and roast in the oven for 10 minutes. Meanwhile, transfer the soup to a blender, process until very smooth, then pass through a sieve. Return to the saucepan to gently heat through (but do not boil) and season to taste with salt (see page 13).

When the potatoes are cooked, remove from the oven and cut in half lengthways. Place on a metal tray skin side up and char until black using a blow torch. Cut each half into 6 pieces and pile neatly in the centre of each of 4 bowls. Put 1 tsp of black olive crumbs over the top and then place a few spoonfuls of lentils on top too. Pour the soup around the pile and eat straight away.

Celeriac (celery root) has gone from an obscure French ingredient to a modern kitchen mainstay in about 10 years. Its flavour is subtle, reminiscent of the celery it is a root of, but sweeter, earthier and more versatile. Its bulk and starch content mean it can form the centre of a meal.

This soup doesn't need much of a garnish – a simple drizzle of hazelnut oil, a scattering of toasted hazelnuts and some salt-baked celeriac cubes (left over from the soup recipe) will do the job. However, if you are making this for a special occasion, then it's worth going the extra mile.

Serves: 4

CELERIAC (CELERY ROOT) SOUP

FOR THE LENTILS

15g (½oz/1½ tbsp) beluga lentils
10g (¼oz/1¼ tbsp) blanched hazelnuts
25ml (1fl oz/5 tsp) hazelnut oil
5ml (1 tsp) lemon juice
1g (scant ¼ tsp) sea salt
2 sprigs of thyme, leaves picked

FOR THE SALT-BAKED CELERIAC (CELERY ROOT)

1 medium celeriac (celery root) (at least 1kg/2¼lb)
100g (3½oz/⅓ cup) fine sea salt

FOR THE SOUP

800ml (28fl oz/3⅓ cups) basic stock (see page 62)
1 bay leaf
1 clove
1 piece of mace
50ml (2fl oz/scant ¼ cup) extra virgin olive oil
2 banana shallots, sliced
2 cloves of garlic, puréed (see page 145)
500g (1lb 2oz) salt-baked celeriac (celery root) (see above)
sea salt
tiny pinch of cayenne pepper

TO SERVE

everyday bread (see page 214)

Soak the beluga lentils a day before cooking them. Place the lentils in a bowl and cover with cold water. Leave overnight.

Make the everyday bread (see page 214) and basic stock (see page 62). Preheat the oven to (fan) 160°C/180°C/350°F/gas mark 4. Line a small baking tray (sheet) with a large sheet of foil – large enough to envelop and seal in the celeriac (celery root). Wash the celeriac (celery root) thoroughly. Pile up the salt on the foil and place the celeriac (celery root) on top. Wrap the foil up around the celeriac (celery root) to form a parcel and bake in the oven for 45 minutes to 2 hours until cooked. After 45 minutes, without unwrapping the celeriac (celery root), check if it's ready by sticking a skewer through it. If it is soft like butter it is ready. If still firm, return to the oven for 15-minute bursts until ready. When cooked, remove the foil and take the celeriac (celery root) off the salt. Set aside and leave until cool enough to handle, then cut away the skin and roots to leave the succulent flesh. Cut the flesh into 2cm (¾-inch) chunks. Weigh 500g (1lb 2oz) and reserve the rest for a garnish.

Now make the lentils. Put the hazelnuts onto a small baking tray (sheet) and roast for 5 minutes. Leave to cool, then cut into chunks roughly twice the size of a lentil. Rinse the lentils and put into a small saucepan with 1 litre (1¾ pints/4 cups) of cold water and 10g (¼oz/1¾ tsp) of salt. Bring to the boil and simmer gently with a lid on for 15 minutes until soft but still holding their shape. Drain and rinse in cold water.

Make the soup. Place the bay leaf, clove and mace in the middle of a 10cm (4-inch) square piece of muslin (cheesecloth). Tie diagonally opposite corners together to form a sealed bag. Heat the olive oil gently in a saucepan. Add the shallots and cook very gently until translucent and soft but not coloured. Add the garlic and cook for a further 3 minutes, then add the celeriac (celery root), stock and the muslin (cheesecloth) parcel and bring to a simmer. Place a lid on and gently simmer for 10 minutes to infuse. Meanwhile, in a small bowl mix the hazelnut oil, lemon and salt together then add the lentils, thyme leaves and hazelnut chunks and set aside.

Remove the soup from the heat and discard the muslin (cheesecloth) bag. Allow the soup to cool slightly and then transfer to a blender. Blend until silky smooth, then pass through a sieve. Add a tiny pinch of cayenne pepper and salt if needed (see page 13). Pour the soup into 4 soup bowls and then drizzle the lentil mix over the top, adding cooked, diced celeriac (celery root) offcuts if you wish. Serve with everyday bread.

Sunchokes are more commonly known as Jerusalem artichokes. Biologically speaking, they are not related to the more striking globe artichokes, although they do share a similar flavour profile. They are actually the root of a sunflower, and my favourite myth behind their naming is that Jerusalem is an English corruption of the Spanish girasol (sunflower), and they were named when they first came to England via Spain, after they took them from the Americas.

I prefer the name sunchoke to Jerusalem artichoke as the latter has developed something of a bad reputation over the years, largely due to the view of it as being peasant animal food. In fact, sunchokes have a wonderful, delicate flavour, refined and elegant – it is such a shame they fell out of favour.

Serves: 4

SUNCHOKE VELOUTÉ
with a mushroom duxelle garnish

FOR THE VELOUTÉ
800ml (28fl oz/3⅓ cups) basic
  stock (see page 62)
500g (1lb 2oz) sunchokes (well
  cleaned)
25ml (1fl oz/5 tsp) extra virgin olive
  oil, plus extra to drizzle
1 banana shallot, sliced
25ml (1fl oz/5 tsp) black truffle oil
sea salt

FOR THE MUSHROOM GARNISH
125g (4½oz) chestnut mushrooms
10ml (2 tsp) extra virgin olive oil
20g (¾oz) peeled and finely diced
  banana shallots
sea salt
25ml (1fl oz/5 tsp) dry white wine

TO SERVE
everyday bread (see page 214).

Make the everyday bread (see page 214) and basic stock (see page 62).

Make the velouté. Fill a bowl with 1 litre (1¾ pints/4 cups) of cold water and add the juice of half a lemon. Using a mandolin, slice the sunchokes quickly and thinly and place straight into the water. Heat the olive oil in a saucepan and add the shallot. Gently fry until just translucent and going soft. Meanwhile, drain the artichokes and pat dry. Add them to the saucepan and fry briefly, then add the stock and bring to the boil. Simmer gently with a lid on for 15–25 minutes until the artichokes are so soft they break between your fingertips. Remove from the heat and allow to cool for 10 minutes.

Next make the mushroom garnish. Chop the mushrooms into 5mm (¼-inch) dice. Heat the olive oil in a small frying pan (skillet) and add the shallots. Cook gently for about 2 minutes until just soft, but not brown. Add the diced mushrooms and a generous pinch of salt and cook until the mushrooms release their juices and these have evaporated. Add the wine and cook until the wine has completely evaporated. Remove the mushrooms from the heat and check and adjust the seasoning (see page 13). Transfer to a small bowl and keep warm while you finish the velouté.

Transfer the velouté to a blender and add the truffle oil and a little salt. Blend until silky smooth and then pass through a sieve. Check and adjust the seasoning (see page 13) and truffle oil flavour, which should not be prominent but should give a richness to the flavour.

Pour the velouté into 4 soup bowls or mugs, add a spoon of the mushroom duxelle to each bowl and a drizzle of olive oil or truffle oil and serve with the everyday bread.

This soup is rich and indulgent and shows off the flavour of the split peas at their best. You don't need to make the garnishes, although they do add another level to the soup. If you just want a nutritious bowl of soup, then simply scatter some fresh thyme and grate a little orange zest over the top when you serve it. If you do include the garnishes you will need to make the orange zest powder at least a day ahead of serving.

Serves: 4

SPLIT PEA SOUP
with salt-baked celeriac (celery root) and orange zaatar

FOR THE SOUP
50g (1¾oz) peeled shallots
50g (1¾oz) peeled carrots
50g (1¾oz) celery
50ml (2fl oz/scant ¼ cup) extra virgin olive oil
5g (⅛ oz) organic ginger (see below), finely sliced
1g (⅓ tsp) turmeric
150g (5½oz/¾ cup) yellow split peas
800ml (28fl oz/3⅓ cups) water
sea salt

FOR THE GARNISH
4 tsp orange zaatar (see page 117)
1 medium celeriac (celery root) (at least 1kg/2¼lb)
rapeseed oil, for frying
8 sprigs of thyme, leaves picked

Prepare the orange zaatar (see page 117) at least a day before making the soup.

Preheat the oven to (fan) 160°C/180°C/350°F/gas mark 4. Cook the celeriac (celery root) following the method for salt-baked celeriac (celery root) on page 55. Chop the peeled celeriac (celery root) into 1.5cm (½-inch) slices and, using a 3cm (1¼-inch) cookie cutter, cut rounds from each slice. You need 4 rounds. Cut each round in half and reserve for later.

Next make the soup. Chop the shallots, carrots and celery to 5mm (¼-inch) dice. Heat half the olive oil in a saucepan and add the diced vegetable mix and ginger. Fry gently, then turn it down to a simmer. Cover with a cartouche (see page 182) and stew very gently for up to 30 minutes, stirring occasionally, until the vegetables are melting and sweet. Remove the cartouche and discard. Add the turmeric and the split peas, stir, then add the measured water. Cover with a lid and simmer gently for 30 minutes until the split peas are completely soft.

Transfer the soup to a blender and add the rest of the olive oil. Process until silky smooth, adding a little water if needed to achieve the texture of thick double cream. Pass through a sieve, season to taste with salt (see page 13) and keep warm.

Heat a little rapeseed oil in a large frying pan (skillet) and add the celeriac (celery root) slices. Fry hard until the celeriac (celery root) is very dark and on the edge of burning on one side only.

Pour the soup into 4 soup bowls. Garnish with 2 celeriac slices and sprinkle 1 teaspoon of orange zaatar mix over the top of each bowl. Sprinkle the thyme leaves over the top, then serve straight away.

GINGER

There are two main types of ginger – the first is the most easily available from supermarkets and is very big and watery and has no real heat or character. The second is the tight, firm variety that tends to be sold as organic in health food shops. It is fiery and punchy and doesn't need peeling. If you can, track down the organic variety for this soup; if you can't then use the supermarket variety but be sure to peel it and use at least double the amount listed here.

This is a recipe I developed from the classic ribollita, the ultimate Italian peasant food. I wanted to create something even more nutritious and a little more elegant than the hearty, lumpy Tuscan bean stew. Don't get me wrong, this is still a rustic meal, but by taking your time and liberally using a really great olive oil you can make one of the most delicious things you eat this year.

Serves: 4

TUSCAN LENTIL & GRAIN BROTH

FOR THE BROTH
100g (3½oz) onion
125g (4½oz) carrot
250g (9oz) celery
75ml (2¾fl oz/⅓ cup) extra virgin
 olive oil
8g (¼oz/1½ tsp) sea salt
4 cloves of garlic
15g (½oz/¼ cup) parsley leaves
2 x 400g (14oz) cans of whole
 plum tomatoes
100g (3½oz/½ cup) puy lentils
85g (3oz/½ cup) barley or spelt
 grain
1 litre (1¾ pints/4 cups) water
125g (4½oz) cavolo nero, cut into
 5mm (¼-inch) strips

TO SERVE
8 tbsp best-quality extra virgin
 olive oil
black pepper
focaccia (see page 218)

Make the focaccia (see page 218).

Dice the onion, carrot and celery into 5mm (¼-inch) cubes. Put the diced vegetables into a saucepan with the olive oil and salt and gently heat. Cook very slowly, taking care not to colour the onions. Chop the garlic and parsley together to create a paste and add to the saucepan. Cook very slowly, for about 30 minutes, until the vegetables are soft.

Meanwhile, empty the cans of tomatoes into a sieve over the sink and gently rinse the sauce from them (see box, below). Shake dry, then cut into 1cm (½-inch) dice. When the vegetables are cooked, add the chopped tomatoes and any juice they released, and continue to cook gently for 20 minutes. Add the lentils, barley and water. Cook gently for about 30 minutes with a lid on, until the barley is plump and soft and the lentils are cooked. If the mix begins to run dry, add a little more water, but not too much — you want a thick broth. Add the cavolo nero and cook gently for another 15 minutes until soft, then remove from the heat. Check the seasoning and adjust if necessary (see page 13).

Spoon the broth into serving bowls and drizzle generously with the best olive oil you can find. Add a twist of black pepper and serve with focaccia.

TINNED TOMATOES

The traditional vegan recipe canon makes liberal use of canned tomatoes. They have a distinctive tomato-ish taste, but with a metallic undertone, and they pop up everywhere. For years I wouldn't go near them, associating them with a style of cookery I was desperate to break away from. Then, by chance, I stumbled on a note in a River Café cookbook that said to wash the sauce from the tomatoes before using them. It turns out the problem with canned tomatoes isn't the actual tomatoes, but the tomato sauce they are kept in. Wash this off and you have a lovely, deep tomato flavour that brings an umami depth (see page 14) without all that messy, funny-tasting sauce nonsense. Just be sure to buy good-quality whole Italian plum tomatoes, as cheap will always taste cheap.

| STOCKS |

BASIC STOCK

This basic stock is built on a foundation of those magic three ingredients: onions, celery and carrot (see box, opposite). Use this recipe as a guide, and build on the basic trio. If it is sunny, I like to use a star anise, if it is raining, I prefer the darker notes of cloves.

If you press down on the vegetables to squeeze the juices you will get the strongest flavour, but your stock will also be cloudy. This is fine if being used in a soup or risotto, but if it is for consommé then you may want to be a little more delicate.

Makes: 1 litre (1¾ pints/4 cups)

1 onion, peeled
1 carrot
1 large stick of celery
¼ slice of lemon
½ fennel bulb
1 star anise
1g (½ tsp) coriander seeds
10 black peppercorns
10g (¼oz/2½ tbsp) parsley (including stalks)
3g (1¼ tbsp) thyme (including stalks)
1 bay leaf
1.2 litres (2 pints/5 cups) water

Slice all the vegetables to a 3mm (⅛ inch) thickness. Place all the ingredients in a saucepan, cover with a lid and gently bring to the boil. Simmer for 5 minutes, then remove from the heat. Allow to cool, then strain through a fine sieve (see introduction, above).

LEEK & GARLIC STOCK

This is a great stock to emphasize the sweet depths of onion in a recipe.

Makes: 1 litre (1¾ pints/4 cups)

1 small leek, finely sliced
2 shallots, finely sliced
2 cloves of garlic, finely sliced
1 clove
1 bay leaf
1 litre (1¾ pints/4 cups) water

Put all the ingredients into a lidded saucepan and gently bring to the boil. Simmer gently for 15 minutes, then remove from the heat and leave for 15 minutes to infuse. Strain through a fine sieve.

MUSHROOM STOCK

Sometimes you need a bit of an umami kick (see page 14) to give your dish a real depth without having to add any big umami ingredients, or maybe you just want to add another layer of umami to give the dish a real punch. If that's your aim, then this is your stock, as it brings a subtle depth that doesn't overwhelm the other flavours on the plate.

As with the basic stock (see opposite), if you press down on the vegetables when straining the stock you will get a stronger flavour, but you will also have a cloudy stock.

Makes: 1 litre (1¾ pints/4 cups)

1 onion, peeled
1 carrot
1 large stick of celery
150g (5½oz) chestnut mushrooms
10 black peppercorns
10g (¼oz/2½ tbsp) parsley (including stalks)
3g (1¼ tbsp) thyme (including stalks)
2 cloves of garlic
1 bay leaf
1.2 litres (2 pints/5 cups) water
15g (½oz) dried porcini mushrooms

Slice the onion, carrot, celery and chestnut mushrooms to a 3mm (⅛ inch) thickness. Put all the ingredients, except the porcini mushrooms, into a lidded saucepan and cover with the measured water. Gently bring to the boil – it should take about 20 minutes to reach boiling point.

Once boiling, simmer very gently for 5 minutes, then remove from the heat. Immediately add the porcini mushrooms, stir to make sure they are submerged, then cover the top of the saucepan tightly with cling film (plastic wrap).

Leave the stock to cool completely, then drain off the stock through a large sieve into a clean saucepan, discarding the vegetables.

MUSHROOM & FENNEL STOCK

This is a great stock that brings a mushroom depth without an overt mushroom flavour. If you want a deeper flavour in your risotto or soup, then substitute this stock for vegetable stock.

Makes: 2 litres (3½ pints/8 cups)

2 onions, finely sliced
4 sticks of celery, finely sliced
2 fennel bulbs, finely sliced
300g (10½oz) white mushrooms, finely sliced
4 cloves of garlic, peeled
2.4 litres (4 pints/10 cups) water
2 bay leaves
4 sprigs of thyme

Put all the ingredients into a lidded saucepan and gently bring to the boil. Simmer gently for 20 minutes, then remove from the heat and leave for 30 minutes. Strain through a fine sieve.

MIREPOIX

If you are a keen cook you will probably have noticed that three vegetables keep popping up together in recipe after recipe – onion, carrot and celery. Look at most vegetable stock recipes and these three are always there. The French call it mirepoix, the Italian name is soffrito. Something about cooking these vegetables together gives the perfect depth and balance of sweetness to any dish. Simmer them in a stock for a light, fresh flavour; or fry them briefly for a sweet, vegetable flavour. Cook them long and slow in oil and something magical happens: the individual character of each vegetable breaks down and a deep, rich sweetness is achieved that is the perfect base for almost any sauce or soup. The trick is to cook them long and slow, making sure they don't dry out. You want them to break down completely – lose your nerve or allow them to colour and something will be missing. You might not know what it is, but your soup will taste decidedly ordinary.

Every recipe is only as good as the ingredients you use, but some recipes are more forgiving than others. This is one of those recipes where the quality of the ingredients used makes a substantial cumulative difference. Using Iranian pistachios (the smaller, dark green variety) will make the pâté richer and a more dramatic shade of green. Finding a buttery olive oil for the pâté will make it rich and satisfying, while using a light, grassy olive oil for the salad, such as one from Sicily, will make it light and fresh. It will, of course, be delicious should you use normal pistachios and a decent olive oil for everything, and more than worth the effort, but it will never reach the subtle, higher levels of perfection that distinguish the great from the good.

Serves: 4

PISTACHIO PÂTÉ
with orange and marjoram salad and carta di musica

FOR THE PÂTÉ
90g (3oz/⅔ cup) Iranian pistachios
90ml (3¼fl oz/generous ⅓ cup)
    top-quality olive oil
15g (½oz/¼ cup) parsley leaves
2g (1 tsp) orange zest
1 clove of garlic
110ml (3¾fl oz/scant ½ cup) cold
    water
3g (scant 1 tsp) agar powder
sea salt
cayenne pepper

**FOR THE ORANGE AND
MARJORAM SALAD**
3 oranges (a sweet seedless variety
    like navel is perfect)
25ml (1fl oz/5 tsp) light, grassy olive
    oil (see introduction)
2g (2 tsp) marjoram leaves,
    shredded
black pepper

FOR THE GARNISH
orange zest powder (see page 117)
carta di musica (see page 210)
4 tsp broken pistachios
few small salad leaves
few marjoram leaves

Make the orange zest powder (see page 117) and the carta di musica (see page 210).

Place a 12cm (4¾-inch) square pastry frame on a small board or plate lined with cling film (plastic wrap) or prepare 4 small pots or cups.

Put the pistachios for the pâté into a blender and process until they resemble fine breadcrumbs. Add the olive oil, parsley, orange zest and garlic and blend until combined. From here on, you need to work fast as the pâté will set quickly as it cools. Put the measured water into a small saucepan and, adding a little at a time, whisk in the agar and bring to the boil, whisking continuously to prevent the agar from catching. As soon as it boils, remove from the heat. Quickly measure the hot agar mix into the blender jug and make it back up to 110ml (3¾fl oz/scant ½ cup) by adding a little cold water if necessary. Blend until silky smooth. Taste for seasoning (see page 13) and add salt and cayenne pepper as necessary, remembering this will be served cold.

Pour the pâté into your prepared mould(s) and then cover the top with cling film (plastic wrap) in contact with the surface of the pâté to prevent a skin from forming. Place in the fridge for at least 2 hours to set firmly.

About 45 minutes before serving, make the salad. Using a sharp knife, remove the orange peel and all the white pith. Cut cleanly down the lines/membranes to remove each segment. Cut the segments into 1cm (½-inch) chunks and put into a bowl with the olive oil, marjoram and a twist of black pepper. Leave for 10–30 minutes for the flavours to come together.

Carefully remove the pâté from the mould (or serve in the pot) and cut into 4 slices. Place a slice on each of 4 starter-sized plates and add a few broken pistachios. Spoon the orange salad in a pile next to the pâté, dust the plate with pinches of orange zest powder and add a few salad and marjoram leaves and the carta di musica.

I have been making this recipe for years. It's known so many iterations it barely resembles its humble origins, but the core is always the same: en papillote carrots, with some simple aromatics, given depth and body by cashew nuts. This version leans a little to the east, but it works well with thyme, rosemary or pine, or even just bay and lemon in place of the ginger and coriander.

If you want to make this recipe without the agar then simply omit it, and the water, from the recipe; however, it won't cut into clean slices without it.

Serves: 4

CARROT & CASHEW PÂTÉ
with rye crisp breads and pickles

20g (¾oz) organic ginger (see page 58), sliced
3g (1½ tsp) coriander seeds
5 star anise
600g (1lb 5oz) peeled and trimmed large carrots
25ml (1fl oz/5 tsp) rapeseed oil
4g (¾ tsp) sea salt
100ml (3½fl oz/scant ½ cup) water (optional)
2g (generous ½ tsp) agar powder (optional)
135g (4¾oz/1 cup) cashew nuts

TO SERVE
rye crisp breads (see page 208)
tamari seeds (see page 20)
pickled carrot (see page 98)
pickled kohlrabi (see page 98)
salad leaves
edible flowers

Make the rye crisp breads (see page 208), tamari seeds (see page 20), pickled carrot (see page 98) and pickled kohlrabi (see page 98).

Preheat the oven to (fan) 160°C/180°C/350°F/gas mark 4. Oil and line a 27 x 5cm (10½ x 2 inch) terrine mould with baking parchment, leaving paper overhanging the edges so you can lift the pâté out. If you are omitting the agar, use 4 pots or tea cups.

Put the ginger, coriander seeds and star anise in a large bowl. Cut the carrots into equal-sized chunks, roughly half the size of the smallest carrot, but don't cut them too small. Add the carrots and oil to the bowl with the ginger. Sprinkle over the salt and mix well. Lay a 45cm (18-inch) length of baking parchment on a chopping board and put the carrot mix in the centre. Fold the paper in half, capturing the carrots in the middle, and roll up the edges to form a sealed half-moon shaped parcel. Place the parcel on a baking tray (sheet) and roast in the oven for 45 minutes until the carrots feel soft. When cooked, remove from the oven and leave to cool slightly.

If using agar, put the water into a small saucepan and whisk gently while slowly sprinkling in the agar. Bring up to a simmer, whisking all the time. When it reaches a gentle boil, remove from the heat and set aside.

Open the bag of carrots and take out the chunks of carrot. Remove and discard all the seeds and ginger, then put the carrots into a blender with the cashews and agar mix (if using). Blend together until very smooth with a silky texture, then pass through a sieve. Taste for salt (see page 13) and adjust as necessary, bearing in mind the mix will be served cold. While hot, spoon or pipe the mix into the prepared terrine mould, banging the mould to knock out any air. Smooth the top with a palette knife and cover with cling film (plastic wrap), in contact with the mix to prevent a skin forming. Place in the fridge for 1–2 hours to set. If made without agar, spoon or pipe it evenly between your pots, place cling film (plastic wrap) over the top in contact with the mix to prevent a skin forming, then place in the fridge for 4 hours to set.

When ready to serve, remove the cling film (plastic wrap) and turn the mould over onto a board. Remove the baking parchment and cut into 1.5cm (½-inch) slices. Serve the pâté with rye crisp breads, pickled kohlrabi, pickled carrot, tamari seeds and a few salad leaves and edible flowers, or spread on a piece of fresh bread with a light green salad for lunch.

This is a simple variation on the carrot & cashew pâté (see page 67), but with bigger, bolder flavours and a nod to northern Europe with the flavour combinations. Beetroot (beets) and carrots are very similar in terms of their structure and their starch and sugar content. The layers you can see in a beetroot (beet) are the same thing as the core and outer of a carrot, just many times over. This means that any technique that works for a carrot will almost certainly work just as well for a beetroot (beet). This pâté is delicious served with rye bread, sauerkraut and mustard.

Serves: 4–6

BEETROOT (BEETS), WALNUT & DILL PÂTÉ
with mustard and sauerkraut

100g (3½oz/1 cup) walnuts
650g (1lb 7oz) red beetroot (beets)
30ml (4fl oz/2 tbsp) water
5g (⅛ oz/1¾ tbsp) dill leaves
20ml (4 tsp) walnut oil
sea salt

TO SERVE
caraway mustard (see page 39)
sauerkraut (see page 99)
sprigs of dill
salad leaves

Make the caraway mustard (see page 39) 3 weeks before eating so it has time to mature, and the sauerkraut (see page 99) at least 5 days before eating.

Put the walnuts in a bowl and cover with cold water by at least 2cm (¾ inch). Leave for 6 hours or ideally overnight to soak.

Preheat the oven to (fan) 160°C/180°C/350°F/gas mark 4. Lay a 45cm (18-inch) length of foil over a deep baking tray (sheet) and put the beetroot (beets) in the centre. Bring the foil up around the beetroot (beets), add the measured water, and roll up the edges to form a sealed parcel. Roast for 45–60 minutes until soft, then remove from the oven and leave until cold. Remove and discard the beetroot (beets) skins. Cut the flesh into chunks and put into a blender. Drain the walnuts, rinse under cold water and add to the blender, along with the dill, walnut oil and a good pinch of salt.

Blend everything together until silky smooth, then ideally pass it through a sieve. Check and adjust the seasoning (see page 13). While the mix is hot, spoon or pipe it into 4–6 pots, covering the surface with cling film (plastic wrap) in contact with the pâté, to prevent a skin forming. Place in the fridge for 1–2 hours to become firm.

When ready, garnish with a sprig of dill and serve with salad leaves, sauerkraut and mustard. This is also delicious spread on rye bread.

The depth of flavour in this parfait is incredible – it's one of those dishes that people can't believe is made purely from plants. The parfait alone is well worth making, set in little pots and served with some crusty bread or carta di musica (see page 210) and a green salad. But if you want something a little more impressive, then adding the port glaze and pea salad really elevates the parfait.

Serves: 4

RICH MUSHROOM PARFAIT
with port glaze and a pea and shallot salad

FOR THE PARFAIT
30g (1¼oz) dried porcini
    mushrooms
300ml (10fl oz/1¼ cups) boiling
    water
40ml (1½fl oz/8 tsp) extra virgin
    olive oil
50g (1¾oz) finely sliced shallots
200g (7oz) finely sliced mushrooms
0.5g (⅔ tsp) thyme leaves
125ml (4fl oz/½ cup) port
1.5g (½ tsp) iota carrageenan
    powder and 1g (scant ¼ tsp) agar
    powder (or 2.5g (¾ tsp) agar
    powder)
100g (3½oz/¾ cup) pine nuts
2g (⅓ tsp) sea salt
10ml (2 tsp) truffle oil

FOR THE GLAZE
80ml (3fl oz/⅓ cup) port
40ml (1½fl oz/8 tsp) red wine
    vinegar
reserved mushroom stock and
    dried mushrooms from the
    parfait (see above)
1g (⅓ tsp) iota carrageenan powder
    (or agar powder)

FOR THE PEA SALAD
50g (1¾oz/⅓ cup) shelled fresh
    peas
12 sugar snap peas, ends and
    strings removed
32 rings of pickled shallots (see
    page 96)
15ml (1 tbsp) extra virgin olive oil
4 little gem lettuce leaves

Put the dried porcini mushrooms and boiling water in a jug to make a stock. Cover with cling film (plastic wrap) and leave for 45 minutes until cold. Sieve the stock, reserving the mushroom stock and two-thirds of the rehydrated mushrooms. Discard the rest of the rehydrated mushrooms.

Seal the base of a 12cm (4¾-inch) square pastry frame (or similar) with cling film (plastic wrap) and place on a small baking tray (sheet). Alternatively, use small moulds or pots.

Put the olive oil into a saucepan and heat gently. Add the shallots and fry until just soft. Add the sliced mushrooms and thyme and cook until the juices from the mushrooms have been released and evaporated. Add the port and cook to reduce to a thick syrup. Add the iota and/or agar to the mix and stir to combine, then add 160ml (5½fl oz/⅔ cup) of the reserved mushroom stock and the rehydrated mushrooms and bring to the boil. Once boiling, remove from the heat and add the pine nuts and salt. Transfer to a blender and blend until very smooth. Add the truffle oil and blend to combine, then adjust the seasoning (see page 13), remembering it will be served cold. Pour into the mould and place in the fridge for at least 2 hours to set.

When the parfait is set, make the port glaze. Put the port and red wine vinegar into a saucepan and heat to reduce by half. Measure the remaining reserved mushroom stock and make it up to 125ml (4fl oz/½ cup). Add it to the saucepan, whisk in the iota and bring to a simmer. Sieve the glaze into a jug and immediately pour over the parfait to an even 2mm (¹⁄₁₆ inch) thickness.

Prepare the pea salad. Blanch the podded peas for 1–2 minutes, then shock in ice-cold water (see page 183). Blanch the sugar snap peas for no longer than 30 seconds, then shock in ice-cold water (see page 183). Drain all the peas and put into a small mixing bowl, then add the pickled shallots and olive oil and mix to dress.

Remove the parfait from the mould and cling film (plastic wrap). Trim the edges then cut into 4 squares with a hot knife. Place 1 piece of parfait on each of 4 plates. Place 1 lettuce leaf next to each parfait and evenly split the pea salad between them, spooning the mix into the lettuce leaf and over the plate. Serve straight away.

I have a quiet love of Germanic flavours: they are so wholesome, robust and honest. They don't have the modern style of the new Nordic foods or the sophistication of the French haute cuisine, but they bring their own comfort and taste. I particularly like to eat them when the leaves begin to fall from the trees.

Remember to allow time for the lentils to soak and the pâté to set. This is also delicious with my fennel and hazelnut salad (see page 102).

Serves: 4–6

GREEN LENTIL & ONION PÂTÉ
with rye bread, sauerkraut and mustard

FOR THE PÂTÉ
160g (5¾oz/¾ cup) dried green
    lentils
100ml (3½fl oz/scant ½ cup)
    rapeseed oil
215g (7½oz) peeled and sliced
    brown onions
4g (¾ tsp) sea salt
30g (1¼oz/½ cup) parsley leaves
30g (1¼oz/1 cup) spinach
4g (1¼ tsp) agar powder (optional)
80ml (3fl oz/⅓ cup) water

TO SERVE
rye bread (see page 207)
sauerkraut (see page 99)
caraway mustard (see page 39)

Make the caraway mustard (see page 39) 3 weeks before you need it so it can mature, and the sauerkraut (see page 99) 5 days before serving.

Put the dried green lentils into a bowl and cover with cold water by at least 2.5cm (1 inch). Put into the fridge and leave to soak for at least 4 hours or overnight.

Make the rye bread (see page 207).

Drain the lentils and rinse under cold water. Put into a small saucepan, cover with cold water (do not add salt), and bring to the boil. Simmer gently until soft but not broken down – you want a pleasing "pop" in the mouth with no grainy texture. Drain and shock with ice-cold water (see page 183) before draining again. Measure out 215g (7½oz) and 80g (3oz) of the cooked lentils and set aside until needed.

Heat the rapeseed oil in a small saucepan and add the onions and salt. Turn down the heat to low and cook gently, stirring often, until they are jelly-like in texture but not coloured. Add the parsley and spinach and turn over to wilt briefly. Add the agar, if using, and stir in thoroughly. Add the water and 215g (7½oz) of the cooked green lentils and heat for about 3 minutes until the lentils are too hot to touch.

Put the lentil and spinach mixture into a blender and process until the mixture is smooth but with flecks of parsley still visible. Working quickly before the agar sets, add the remaining 80g (3oz) of cooked lentils to the mix and stir to combine. Spoon into 4–6 glass containers and cover with cling film (plastic wrap) to prevent a skin from forming. Put into the fridge for 4 hours to set.

Serve the pâté, spread on rye bread, with sauerkraut and mustard.

Every variety of squash and pumpkin is like a vegetable in its own right. It isn't possible to simply swap them between recipes unless they are closely related. Having said that, because this recipe is blended you do have a lot more room to adapt. The main thing that will make a difference is water content: very wet varieties like muscat de Provence will give a very loose liquid purée and you should try and cook as much liquid out as possible; very dry varieties, like Crown Prince, will probably need a little water adding to get a good texture. You're going to have to get to know your ingredient here and use your instincts as you go.

Serves: 4

SQUASH AND HAZELNUT PÂTÉ

1.2kg (2½lb) dry squash variety (such as Crown Prince) (peeled and trimmed weight), cut into 2cm (¾-inch) cubes
50ml (2fl oz/scant ¼ cup) rapeseed oil
100g (3½oz) blanched hazelnuts
25ml (1fl oz/5 tsp) hazelnut oil
6 sprigs of thyme
cayenne pepper
sea salt

Preheat the oven to (fan) 160°C/180°C/350°F/gas mark 4.

Toss the cubes of squash with the rapeseed oil and a little salt, spread out on a lined baking tray and roast in the oven for about 40 minutes, until soft and beginning to char on the edges.

Put the hazelnuts on a baking tray and roast them for 7 minutes or until they are a dark golden-brown colour.

Remove the squash from the oven and leave to cool. Remove 450g (1lb) of the roasted squash for the pâté and reserve the rest for scattering at the end.

Pick the thyme leaves from the sprigs and put into the blender along with the cooked squash, roasted nuts, hazelnut oil and a little cayenne and salt. Blend until silky smooth.

Depending on the variety of squash and the type of oven you are using, you may need to add a splash of water to get the mix moving. Taste and check the seasoning, adjusting if needed (see page 13).

Pour into a tub for storage; the pâté will store for up to 3 days in the refrigerator, as will the reserved squash pieces.

There are two ways of treating asparagus: as a fresh, green vegetable like peas; or for a darker flavour experience, like a cabbage. If you want it fresh, simply blanch and enjoy with something tart such as lemon aioli. If you treat it like a cabbage, then you're best off charring it (see the Maillard reaction, page 175). This recipe makes liberal use of the cabbage connection, and coupled with onions and dark spring greens it's as far from the fresh green version as you can get – it's also seductively delicious.

Serves: 4

CHARRED ASPARAGUS
with a cannelini bean and onion purée

FOR THE BEAN PURÉE
100g (3½oz) finely sliced brown
    onions
25ml (1fl oz/5 tsp) extra virgin
    olive oil
100g (3½oz/½ cup) cooked
    cannellini beans (good-quality
    canned beans are fine)
25ml (1fl oz/5 tsp) best-quality
    (preferably Italian) extra virgin
    olive oil
20ml (4 tsp) lemon juice
sea salt

FOR THE ASPARAGUS PARCELS
20 asparagus spears
4 large spring green leaves
rapeseed oil, to fry

FOR THE GARNISH
20 pickled shallot rounds (see
    page 96)
cabbage powder (see page 116)

Make the pickled shallots (see page 96) and cabbage powder (see page 116) in advance. The purée is also best made the day before you need it.

To make the purée, heat the onions and regular extra virgin olive oil in a small saucepan. Stew gently for about 25 minutes until the onions are meltingly soft but not coloured, then transfer to a blender and add the cannellini beans, best-quality olive oil and lemon juice. Season well with salt and blend for 3–4 minutes until silky smooth. Check and adjust the seasoning (see page 13). Transfer to an airtight container and store in the fridge for at least 4 hours to firm up. (The purée will keep in the fridge for up to 3 days.) When ready to cook, transfer the purée into a piping bag and leave to come to room temperature.

Blanch the asparagus for 2 minutes and shock in ice-cold water (see page 183). Blanch the spring green leaves for 30 seconds and shock in ice-cold water (see page 183). Cut 4 x 1cm (½-inch) wide strips from the spring green leaves, each long enough to wrap around 5 asparagus spears. Separate the asparagus into 4 piles of 5 spears and wrap each pile together using 1 spring green strip for each parcel – the strip should just stick to itself.

Heat a splash of rapeseed oil in a large frying pan (skillet) until smoking hot. Add the asparagus parcels and fry hard on one side until very dark in colour and burnt in places. Carefully turn over and colour on each side until they are evenly coloured all round.

Place 1 asparagus parcel onto each of 4 starter-size plates. Pipe about 3 tablespoons of the cannellini bean purée into a neat pile next to the asparagus and arrange 5 of the pickled shallot rings on each plate.

Put the cabbage powder into the centre of a 20cm (8-inch) square piece of muslin (cheesecloth), bring the corners together to form a parcel and tie it to form a shaker, or use a small, fine sieve. Sprinkle the cabbage powder over the bean purée and around the plate, then serve straight away.

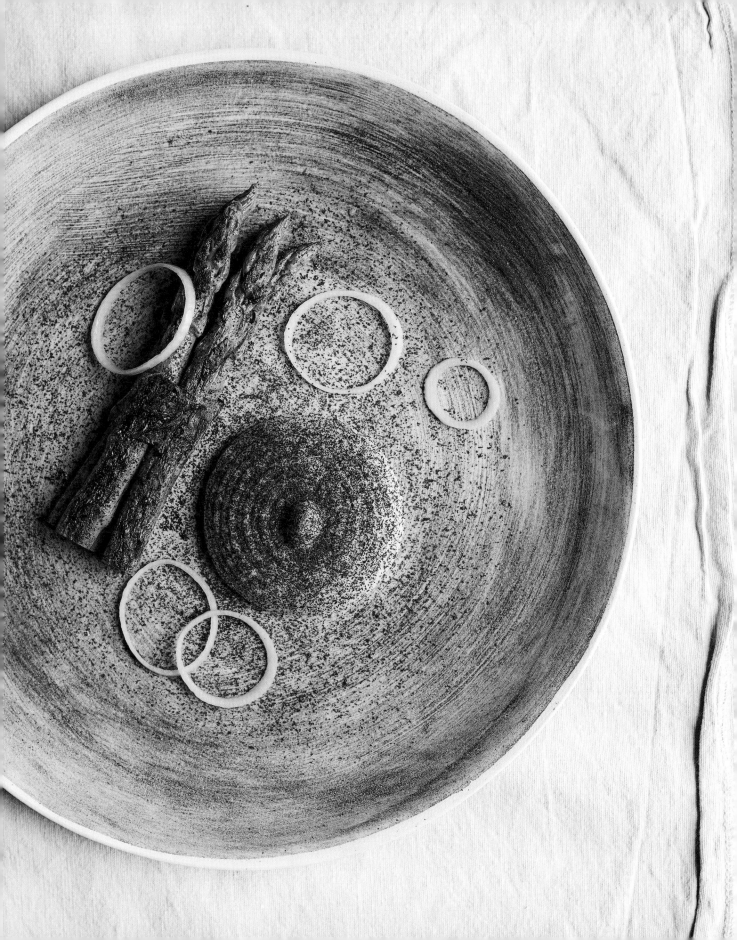

In an ideal world you would cook the charred leeks on a barbecue. The outer leaves of the leeks burn and protect the inner layers that cook slowly and become melting and sweet. You can create a similar effect with a griddle pan – just make sure you have the kitchen extractor fan on full! This recipe makes a romesco which has a dip/spread consistency. To make more of a sauce, you can thin it out with a little water or olive oil. I make it in a pestle and mortar as I like the rustic texture, but you can make it in a food processor if you prefer. Omit the breadcrumbs if you want to make it gluten free.

Serves: A generous starter for 4

CHARRED BABY LEEKS
with romesco sauce

FOR THE ROMESCO SAUCE
4 red (bell) peppers
110g (3¾oz) almonds
3 cloves of garlic
8g (¼oz) dried Aleppo chilli flakes
20g (¾oz) breadcrumbs (optional)
50ml (2fl oz/scant ¼ cup) sherry
    vinegar
100ml (3½fl oz/scant ½ cup) extra
    virgin olive oil, plus extra for
    roasting the peppers
sea salt

FOR THE CHARRED LEEKS
8–12 baby leeks

Preheat the oven to (fan) 160°C/180°C/350°F/gas mark 4.

To roast the peppers, cut a slit in the side of each one and rub with a little olive oil. Roast in the oven on a baking tray (sheet) until charred and black. Remove from the oven, put them straight into a bowl and cover with a plate until cool. Peel off the skins and remove the seeds.

Put the almonds on a small baking tray (sheet) and roast in the oven for 7 minutes, until golden brown.

Working in batches, depending on the size of your pestle and mortar, combine the ingredients in the following order: grind the garlic to a paste with a little salt, roughly chop the peppers and grind to a coarse paste with the garlic, then add the chilli flakes and mix. Add the toasted almonds and grind to rough breadcrumb size before adding the breadcrumbs (if using) and grinding it all to a pesto-like consistency. Add the vinegar and mix, then mix in the oil and season with salt to taste (see page 13).

To make the charred leeks, heat a barbecue or large griddle pan until very hot. Add the leeks and leave until the underside begins to blacken. Turn them over by a quarter and repeat. Keep turning them over by a quarter until the whole leek is blackened and the inside is melting, then remove from the heat and allow to cool slightly. Cut off the outer charred layer and peel away, leaving just the succulent soft middle.

Serve the leeks with the romesco sauce. Delicious with a crusty loaf of bread and a robust red wine.

Courgettes (zucchini) are one of my favourite vegetables, both to eat and grow. Nurture one plant and you'll have more than you can eat all through the season. This dish makes use of courgettes (zucchini) when they are, in my opinion, best to eat – small and sweet, no bigger than your forefinger. If they are bigger than this, then you'll have to trim them down to smaller pieces, perhaps into batons. Either way, this is a fresh, delicious plate of summer.

Serves: 4

FINGERLING COURGETTES (ZUCCHINI)
with lemon and mint ice and garden herb purée

FOR THE LEMON AND MINT ICE

100g (3½oz/½ cup) caster (superfine) sugar
250ml (8½fl oz/1 cup) water
35g (1¼oz/1½ cups) mint leaves
80ml (3fl oz/⅓ cup) lemon juice

FOR THE HERB PURÉE

175ml (6fl oz/¾ cup) extra virgin olive oil
150g (5½oz) banana shallots, sliced
100g (3½oz/3⅓ cups) spinach, coarsely chopped
50g (1¾oz/1 cup) chives, coarsely chopped
100g (3½oz/1⅔ cups) parsley leaves, coarsely chopped
50ml (2fl oz/scant ¼ cup) cold water
10ml (2 tsp) black truffle oil
sea salt

FOR THE CHARRED COURGETTES (ZUCCHINI)

12 finger-sized courgettes (zucchini), with flowers if possible
60ml (2¼fl oz/¼ cup) extra virgin olive oil
2 cloves of garlic, peeled and cut in half lengthways

First make the lemon and mint ice as it needs 4 hours to freeze. Put the sugar and water into a small saucepan and bring to the boil, then remove from the heat and add the mint. Leave to infuse until it cools to room temperature, then add the lemon juice. Pass through a sieve into a small container and freeze for 4 hours (or until frozen solid). Use a fork to scrape the ice into a fine powder/mushy texture. Return to the freezer.

To make the purée, heat 25ml (1fl oz/5 tsp) of the olive oil in a large saucepan. Add the shallots and cook until soft and translucent. Add the spinach, chives and parsley and stir until the spinach has wilted, then tip onto a large baking tray (sheet), spread out and leave to cool. Once cool, transfer to a blender. Add the water and the rest of the olive oil and blend until smooth and glossy (don't add extra water). Once completely smooth, add the truffle oil and blend to mix. Pass through a sieve into a bowl and season to taste (see page 13). Cover with cling film (plastic wrap) in contact with the surface to prevent a skin forming and place in the fridge to chill.

Remove the courgette (zucchini) flowers, pinch out the stamen and discard, and set aside. Blanch the courgettes (zucchini) for 3–5 minutes, until just softening, then shock in ice-cold water (see page 183). Pat dry, then cut each courgette (zucchini) in half lengthways. Heat the olive oil in a saucepan and add the garlic. Cook gently for 2 minutes, then turn down the heat. Add the halved courgettes (zucchini) and heat very gently without frying until warm.

Pour a little of the herb purée in a round blob on each plate and add 6 courgette (zucchini) pieces and add 1 tablespoon of lemon mint ice. Tear the reserved courgette (zucchini) flowers into strips and scatter across each plate. Serve straight away.

Red peppers can be a tricky ingredient to use. They are delicious, sweet and succulent, but they can also lack a level of sophistication, and their sweetness is almost too much when they are central to a dish. Here I have used the earthy flavour of broad beans (fava beans) and garlic to balance them.

Serves: 4

ROASTED RED PEPPERS
with broad beans (fava beans) and stewed tomatoes

**FOR THE BROAD BEANS
(FAVA BEANS)**

100g (3½oz/⅔ cup) whole dried
    broad beans (fava beans)
400g (14oz) plum tomatoes
4g (¾ tsp) sea salt
60ml (2¼fl oz/¼ cup) extra virgin
    olive oil
50g (1¾oz) spring onions
    (scallions), finely sliced
10g (¼oz/2⅔ tbsp) parsley leaves,
    finely chopped
2g (scant 1 tsp) smoked paprika
10ml (2 tsp) red wine vinegar
100g (3½oz/3⅓ cups) baby spinach
    leaves

FOR THE PEPPERS

1 x quantity of broad bean (fava
    bean) purée (see page 182)
4 Romano red peppers
2g (1 tsp) fennel seeds
extra virgin olive oil
sea salt

FOR THE GARNISH

2 spring onions (scallions),
    finely sliced
8 pitted green olives, sliced
parsley leaves
extra virgin olive oil, to drizzle
black pepper

First soak the beans. Put the whole broad beans (fava beans) into a small bowl and cover with cold water by at least 2cm (¾ inch). Leave to soak for at least 6 hours or ideally overnight. Soak the split broad beans (fava beans) for the broad bean (fava bean) purée (see page 182).

Preheat the oven to (fan) 160°C/180°C/350°F/gas mark 4. Cut the top off the Romano red peppers, then cut in half lengthways and remove and discard the seeds. Place the halved peppers in a bowl. Add the fennel seeds, a good glug of olive oil and a few pinches of salt and mix well. Place a 60cm (24-inch) strip of baking parchment on a baking tray (sheet) and place the peppers in the middle. Fold the paper in half and roll up the edges to make a sealed parcel. Bake for 30 minutes until soft, then leave to cool. Remove from the bag and discard the juice.

Drain and rinse the whole broad beans (fava beans) in cold water, then put into a small saucepan with 500ml (18fl oz/2 cups) of cold water. Bring to the boil and simmer for 45 minutes until soft but not broken up, adding more water if necessary. Once cooked, drain and rinse. Meanwhile, prepare the broad bean (fava bean) purée (see page 182).

Remove the stem of each plum tomato, then cut a cross in the skin at the bottom. Blanch the tomatoes in boiling water until the skin starts to split, then shock in ice-cold water (see page 183). Peel off the skins, cut each tomato in half and discard the seeds. Chop into 7mm (⅓ inch) dice. Put the tomatoes, salt and olive oil into a large frying pan (skillet) and simmer gently for 5 minutes. Add the spring onion (scallion) and simmer until the tomatoes have broken down, then add the parsley and broad beans (fava beans.) Simmer gently to warm. Add the smoked paprika and vinegar and stir to combine. Set aside.

Lay the pepper halves out and spread a thin layer of the broad bean (fava bean) purée down the middle, stopping 2cm (¾ inch) from the top and bottom. Roll each pepper up lengthways into a tight spiral. Cut each pepper in half widthways and place the pieces, cut side up, on a lined baking tray (sheet). Drizzle with a little olive oil and place in the oven for 10 minutes to heat.

Gently reheat the tomato and broad bean (fava bean) mixture and add the spinach, folding it over gently until the spinach is just wilted, then remove from the heat. Check and adjust the seasoning (see page 13).

Put a quarter of the bean mix on each of 4 starter-sized plates. Arrange 4 rolls of roasted pepper on each plate. Sprinkle with the spring onions (scallions), green olives and parsley leaves and add a drizzle of olive oil and a twist of black pepper. Serve straight away.

This dish is all about the subtle textures. Yes, the flavours are bold and clear, but it is the soft bite of the beetroot (beet) slivers with the creamy cashews and the crunch of the pickled beetroot (beets) that makes it stand out. It's a great dish, simple, clean and delicious. Just allow two days to make the cashew purée.

If you want to make a larger meal, then toss the beetroot (beet) slivers with some light salad leaves, thin the cashew purée to a thick cream consistency with water, and drizzle it all over, using the vierge as the salad dressing, then serve it with a slice of sourdough for a nutritious lunch.

Serves: 4

CHIOGGIA BEETROOT (BEET) SLIVERS
with aged cashew purée and lavender beetroot (beet) vierge

FOR THE CASHEW PURÉE
250g (9oz/2 cups) cashew nuts
2.5g (1 tsp) onion powder
   (see page 116)
1 acidophilus capsule
200ml (7fl oz/generous ¾ cup)
   water
5g (⅛ oz/1 tsp) sea salt

FOR THE VIERGE DRESSING
1g (½ tsp) coriander seeds
50ml (2fl oz/scant ¼ cup) lavender
   oil (see page 220)
20ml (4 tsp) lemon juice
10 tarragon leaves, diced
15–20g (½–¾oz) pickled beetroot
   (beets) (see page 96), diced

FOR THE BEETROOT (BEET) SLIVERS
2 large Chioggia beetroots (beets)
   (or 4 small)
1 clove
2g (1 tsp) coriander seeds
2g (1 tsp) black peppercorns
10g (¼oz) tarragon
5g (⅛ oz) sprigs of thyme
2 bay leaves
10g (¼oz/1¾ tsp) sea salt
100ml (3½fl oz/scant ½ cup) cold
   water

FOR THE GARNISH
selection of small salad leaves

You will need to prepare the cashew purée over 2 days. Put the cashews in a small bowl, cover with cold water and leave to soak for 2 hours. Prepare the pickled beetroot (beets) (see page 96) and onion powder (see page 116).

Strain the cashews, place in a blender and add the contents of the acidophilus capsule and the water. Blend to a very smooth paste, then put into a sterilized (see page 99) lidded container. Leave somewhere warm (22°C/71°F) for 24 hours. When ready, it should smell sweet and sharp and have a foamy texture. If it isn't ready, leave for a further 12–24 hours. (If it smells rancid or has developed mould you'll have to start again.)

Make the vierge dressing at least 2 hours before serving. Crush the coriander seeds using a pestle and mortar, then put all the vierge ingredients, except the diced pickled beetroot (beets), into a small saucepan and bring to the boil. Pour this over the beetroot (beets) dice and leave for 2 hours, then strain.

When the fermented cashew is ready, place it in the blender with the salt and onion powder and blend until very smooth. Transfer to the fridge.

Preheat the oven to (fan) 160°C/180°C/350°F/gas mark 4. Take a large sheet of foil and place a similar sized sheet of baking parchment on top. Put both on a baking tray (sheet). Wash the beetroots (beets) carefully. Place the clove, coriander seeds, peppercorns, tarragon, thyme, bay leaves and salt on the centre of the baking parchment and the beetroots (beets) on top. Half form a parcel so liquid cannot escape, then pour over the measured water. Seal the parcel tightly. Place in the oven and bake for 35 minutes, then remove from the oven and open the parcel. Check the beetroot (beets) are tender – a knife should pass through them easily. If they are not ready, return to the oven in 15-minute bursts until done. Allow to cool in the parcel, then rub off the skin and discard. Set a mandolin to a 7mm (⅓ inch) setting and carefully slice the beetroots (beets) into slivers (don't worry if they break up a little bit).

Place 2 tablespoons of cashew purée on each of 4 starter-sized plates and then swipe each blob with the back of the spoon. Split the beetroot (beet) slices into 4 portions and then split each pile in 3, there should be 4–6 slices (no more) in each pile. Carefully fold each pile over like a taco and place 3 piles along the centre of the plate between the cashew purée. Arrange salad leaves in among this and then dress the whole dish with the vierge and garnish with salad leaves. Serve immediately.

The ajo blanco provides a wonderful, zingy foil for the deep flavour of the burnt spring greens. I sieve the ajo blanco to a smooth consistency so it resembles a sauce more than the traditional soup in order to make this rustic peasant dish refined and elegant. However, if you want your meal a little heartier, then sieve it a little coarser, or, for the full rustic experience, not at all.

The ajo blanco is best made a day before eating (you will therefore need to soak the almonds two days ahead) to allow the garlic and vinegar to mellow – if you serve it when you've just made it the garlic will be very strong and pronounced.

Serves: 4

BURNT SUMMER BEAN PARCEL
with confit potatoes and ajo blanco

FOR THE AJO BLANCO
200g (7oz/1½ cups) whole almonds
2 cloves of garlic, peeled, cut in half and stem removed
350ml (12fl oz/1½ cups) cold water
100ml (3½fl oz/scant ½ cup) extra virgin olive oil
25ml (1fl oz/5 tsp) sherry vinegar
5g (⅛ oz/1 tsp) sea salt

FOR THE CONFIT POTATOES
200g (7oz) new potatoes
2g (⅓ tsp) sea salt
good-quality olive oil

FOR THE SPRING GREEN PARCELS
2 brown onions, thinly sliced
50ml (2fl oz/scant ¼ cup) extra virgin olive oil
2g (⅓ tsp) sea salt
6g (⅛ oz/1⅓ tbsp) chopped summer savory (or 7g (¼ oz/ 2¾ tbsp) chopped tarragon)
4 large, dark, spring green leaves
40 untrimmed green beans
rapeseed oil, to fry

FOR THE GARNISH
1 x quantity of spring green crisps (see page 26)

Soak the almonds 2 days in advance of cooking. Put 150g (5½oz/1 cup) of the almonds into a small bowl and cover with cold water by at least 2cm (¾ inch). Put into the fridge and leave overnight.

Preheat the oven to (fan) 160°C/180°C/350°F/gas mark 4. Place the remaining almonds on a baking tray (sheet) and roast in the oven for 8 minutes.

Drain and rinse the soaked almonds, then put all the ajo blanco ingredients into a blender and process for 1–2 minutes until completely smooth and creamy. Line a sieve with a 45cm (18-inch) square piece of muslin (cheesecloth) set over a jug. Pour the almond mix into the muslin (cheesecloth) and collect up the corners to make a bag. Squeeze to extract the ajo blanco into the jug. Keep squeezing until you are struggling to get much liquid out, then discard the bag. (The ajo blanco will keep in the fridge for up to 3 days.)

Make the spring green crisps (see page 26).

Trim the new potatoes into neat, squared-off shapes, removing the skin as you do so, then chop into 5mm (¼-inch) dice. Mix with the salt and leave for 30 minutes until a little juice is released. Drain off the liquid and put the potatoes in a small saucepan. Just cover with olive oil and simmer very gently over a low heat for about 10 minutes until the potatoes are just soft, checking them regularly. Strain the potatoes from the oil and allow the potatoes to cool to room temperature.

Make the filling for the parcels. Put the onions, olive oil and salt into a small saucepan and heat very gently until the onions are soft but not coloured. Spread out on a plate and leave to cool completely. Once cold, mix in the summer savory.

Trim the spring green leaves and then cut the central stem out, leaving 8 large half-strips of leaf. Blanch the spring green leaves for 30 seconds, then shock in ice-cold water (see page 183). Blanch the green beans for 2 minutes, then shock in ice-cold water (see page 183). Dry the beans and spring green leaves with kitchen (paper) towel. Select the best 4 spring green leaves.

continued on next page>>

<< continued from previous page

HIGH PROTEIN SAUCES

Putting vegetables at the centre of the plate creates beautiful, elegant and delicious food, but it can leave more traditional diners asking where the protein is. Leaving aside the fact that, per calorie, many plants have more protein than meats, one of my favourite tricks is to use high-calorie and high-protein foods in sauces and garnishes, inverting the traditional hierarchy of nutrients. The Mediterranean is a wonderful inspiration for this idea, with a treasure trove of traditional sauces made from nuts and seeds, from romesco and pesto to this wonderful cold soup made from almonds, garlic and olive oil.

Lay 1 leaf across a chopping board with the straight edge towards the top. Place 10 green beans in a pile on the leaf with the stalk end just sticking over the bottom, uneven edge of the leaf by about 5mm (¼ inch) and the pointed end extending at least 2cm (¾ inch) over the top. Trim the leaf if necessary.

Place a tablespoon of the onion mix on top of the pile of beans. Fold over one side of the leaf and then tightly roll the beans into a parcel, a little like sushi, to form a very tight bundle with the beans sticking out of the top and bottom. The leaf should stick to itself and hold the parcel together. Trim the parcel at the bottom to remove the bottom of the stalks and leave a clean crisp edge. Set to one side and repeat 3 more times.

Heat a little rapeseed oil in a frying pan (skillet) until very hot, almost smoking. Place the parcels in the pan with the sealed flap on the bottom, pressing them down to flatten against the pan. Fry very hard until the cabbage is almost burnt. Do not fiddle with them, you do not want to risk them falling apart. Carefully turn them over and repeat on the other side.

Place 1 parcel in the centre of each of 4 small bowls. Pile a tablespoon of confit potatoes next to the parcel, add the ajo blanco and lay a spring green crisp across the top.

This dish is an example of how to take the most humble of ingredients and raise it to the uppermost heights with careful presentation and premium treatment. Donkey carrots are the large, misshapen carrots most supermarkets reject, but they are the sweetest of the carrots and cost almost nothing.

This is a very involved dish with multiple components that require two days of preparation, but the end result is a dish that makes the humble rejected carrot taste like the finest thing you have ever eaten.

Serves: 4

ROASTED DONKEY CARROTS
with cashew cheese and seeded buckwheat

FOR THE CASHEW CHEESE
250g (9oz/2 cups) cashew nuts
3 acidophilus capsules
25ml (1fl oz/5 tsp) water
10ml (2 tsp) extra virgin olive oil
4g (¾ tsp) sea salt
10g (¼oz/scant ¼ cup) chives, finely sliced
10g (¼oz/2⅔ tbsp) parsley leaves, very finely chopped

FOR THE BUCKWHEAT
50g (1¾oz/⅓ cup) hulled buckwheat
30ml (1fl oz/2 tbsp) rapeseed oil
20g (¾oz/2½ tbsp) sunflower seeds

FOR THE ROASTED CARROTS
0.1g (pinch) saffron
40ml (1½fl oz/8 tsp) boiling water
4 large, organic donkey carrots, washed thoroughly
2 star anise
1g (½ tsp) coriander seeds
25ml (1fl oz/5 tsp) extra virgin olive oil
3g (½ tsp) sea salt, plus extra to sprinkle
rapeseed oil, to fry
truffle oil, to drizzle

FOR THE GARNISH
20 strips of pickled carrot (see page 98)
black truffle, grated (optional)

First prepare the cashew cheese as it takes 2 days to make. Put the cashews in a small bowl and cover with cold water. Leave for 2 hours (no longer), then drain and place in a blender with the contents of the acidophilus capsules. Add the measured water and olive oil and blend. If too dry, add just a little more water – you need a firm mix you can shape. Line a sieve with a muslin (cheesecloth) and set it over a bowl. Add the cashew mix, then fold the muslin (cheesecloth) over and cover it with cling film (plastic wrap). Leave somewhere warm (22°C/71°F) for 24 hours, until it smells sweetly sour and 'cheesy'. Transfer the cashew cheese mix to a blender and process until smooth, then place in an airtight container in the fridge for 4 hours to firm up. Prepare the pickled carrot (see page 98).

When the cheese has chilled, add the salt and mix well, then transfer to a piping bag with a 1.5cm (½-inch) round nozzle (tip). Put the chives and parsley onto a plate and mix together. Pipe a 10cm (4-inch) long sausage of the cashew mix onto the herbs and gently roll it, taking care not to damage its shape.

Lay out a 15cm (6-inch) long strip of cling film (plastic wrap) and, using a palette knife, transfer the cashew sausage onto it. Carefully fold the cling film (plastic wrap) over and roll the sausage tightly in it. Twist one end and then the other to tighten the shape, taking care not to trap any air inside. Put the sausage into the fridge and repeat with the mix, piping and rolling until you have 4 sausages. Leave these in the fridge for 24 hours to become really firm. (Any leftover mix makes a great spread on toast.)

Put the buckwheat into a bowl and cover with cold water. Leave to soak for 2 hours, then drain and rinse. Fill a saucepan with 2 litres (3½ pints/8 cups) of water and 20g (¾oz/1¼ tbsp) of salt and bring to the boil. Add the buckwheat and cook for 3–5 minutes until just softening (be careful not to overcook it). Drain and rinse in cold water, then set aside.

Put the saffron into a small bowl and pour the boiling water over it. Leave for 30 minutes. Preheat the oven to (fan) 160°C/180°C/350°F/gas mark 4.

Cut 6 diagonal scores 5mm (¼ inch) deep along one side of a carrot. Turn over and repeat on the other side. Repeat with the rest of the carrots. Take a 45cm (18-inch) length of baking parchment and lay it across a deep baking tray (sheet). Lay the carrots across the middle of the paper and add the rest of the roasted carrots ingredients except the rapeseed oil and truffle oil. Mix together and then fold the bag over and roll up the edges to form a sealed parcel. Bake in the oven for 45 minutes to 1 hour until the carrots are meltingly soft but not coloured.

Allow the carrots to cool completely in the bag, then remove them from the aromatic mix. Cut each carrot in half lengthways. Turn down the oven to (fan) 140°C/160°C/310°F/gas mark 2½.

Take each half of carrot and lay it flat, face up, in front of you. Using a sharp knife, cut scores diagonally all along it approximately 4mm (¼ inch) apart and 4mm (¼ inch) deep. Then cut scores diagonally in the other direction to form a cross hatch. Repeat this for all the halves.

Heat a little rapeseed oil in a large frying pan (skillet) until very hot. Add the carrot halves, in batches if necessary, and press down firmly so the whole face is in contact with the pan. When almost blackened, place on a small baking tray (sheet), face down, and put in the oven for 5 minutes to warm through fully. After 5 minutes, remove from the oven and turn the carrots face up. Sprinkle a little salt over each one and then drizzle generously with truffle oil, flexing each carrot slightly to open up the cross hatch.

Heat the rapeseed oil for the buckwheat in a small frying pan (skillet). Add the sunflower seeds and fry gently until a dark golden colour but not burnt. Add the cooked buckwheat and stir to mix and warm through.

Place 1 piece of carrot on each of 4 plates. Remove the cling film (plastic wrap) from each cashew "sausage" (rolling it gently to re-form the shape if necessary) and place the "sausage" next to the carrot along with a couple of tablespoons of buckwheat. Add 5 rolls of pickled carrot, and, if using, grate black truffle generously across the carrot. Serve immediately.

This recipe plays on the idea that Jerusalem artichokes and sunflower seeds are both from the sunflower family. The artichokes are the root and the seeds are, well, the seed. As is so often the case with members of the same family, the flavours go wonderfully together, balanced by the bitter acidity of the grapefruit. This recipe comes courtesy of Steven Yates.

Serves: 4–6

ROAST JERUSALEM ARTICHOKES
with sunflower seed purée and pink grapefruit gel

FOR THE ARTICHOKES
8 Jerusalem artichokes
2 bay leaves
5g (⅛ oz/2 tbsp) thyme leaves
5g (⅛ oz/1 tsp) sea salt, plus extra
    to sprinkle
20ml (4 tsp) rapeseed oil
sunflower oil, for frying and
    deep-fat frying

FOR THE GRAPEFRUIT GEL
4g (generous 1 tsp) agar powder
40g (1½oz/3⅓ tbsp) caster
    (superfine) sugar
190ml (6½fl oz/generous ¾ cup)
    pink grapefruit juice
25ml (1fl oz/5 tsp) white wine

FOR THE PURÉE
1 x quantity of sunflower seed
    purée (see page 183)

FOR THE GRAPEFRUIT SEGMENTS
1–2 pink grapefruit

FOR THE GARNISH
micro red sorrel

Preheat the oven to (fan) 160°C/180°C/350°F/gas mark 4. Clean the artichokes thoroughly with a brush. Lay out a 45cm (18-inch) length of baking parchment and put the artichokes into the centre. Scatter the rest of the artichoke ingredients (except the sunflower oil) over the artichokes. Fold the paper in half capturing the ingredients in the middle and roll up the edges, to form a sealed half-moon shaped parcel.

Place the parcel on a small baking tray (sheet) and roast for 20–30 minutes until the artichokes feel soft when pushed through the outside of the bag, but aren't coloured. Allow the bag to cool for 5 minutes and then carefully open and remove the artichokes. Cut each artichoke in half lengthways, pat dry and sprinkle with a pinch of salt. Reserve 2 roasted artichokes to make artichoke crisps.

Make the sunflower seed purée (see page 183). Make the grapefruit gel. Mix the agar with the sugar. Put the grapefruit juice and white wine into a small saucepan and whisk the sugar and agar mix in slowly. Put the saucepan onto the heat and gently bring to a simmer, whisking to stop the agar from sticking. As soon as it starts to simmer, remove from the heat and pour into a small container. Cover and put into the fridge for 30 minutes. Once set firmly, transfer to a small blender and blend until completely smooth. Transfer to a piping bag.

Prepare the grapefruit segments. Using a sharp knife, peel off the grapefruit skin and white pith. Cut cleanly down each side of the membranes, working round the fruit to remove each segment (you need 3 per person), then place on kitchen (paper) towel. Spread the grapefruit segments out on a metal tray and, using a blowtorch, burn the upward face (you can skip this step but it is a nice touch).

Prepare your deep-fat fryer (see page 24). Cut the 2 reserved roasted artichokes in half lengthways and scoop as much flesh out as you can. Fry the skins until golden brown, then drain on kitchen (paper) towel and sprinkle with a little salt.

Heat a little rapeseed oil in a frying pan (skillet) until very hot. Put the artichokes face down in the pan and cook until very well done but not quite burnt.

Put 2 tablespoons of sunflower seed purée on each of 4 starter-size plates and spread it out slightly, then spread the purée across the plate in one confident motion. Add the roasted artichokes and grapefruit segments on top of the purée. Dot pink grapefruit gel around the plate and add red sorrel leaves and an artichoke crisp. Serve straight away.

| PICKLES |

Traditionally pickling was used as a way of preserving crops for the winter, but in today's world of easily available ingredients year round there is little need unless you have your own garden. This tradition has left us with a wonderful culinary tool; pickles add acidity, sweetness and texture to a plate, helping to balance dishes, particularly when they are very fatty or rich.

Traditional pickles are designed to preserve food without refrigeration and so are very high in acidity, and/or sugar, and this can present a problem when balancing delicate plates of food, or pairing them with wine. I tend to water down the pickling liquid to give a more refined taste and to make matching with wine easier, but this does affect the preserving function of the liquid. Be sure to keep these pickles in the fridge so they don't spoil.

PICKLED CAULIFLOWER

Makes: 250ml (8½fl oz) jar

30g (1¼oz) cauliflower florets, about 1cm (½ inch) long
50g (1¾oz/¼ cup) caster (superfine) sugar
150ml (5fl oz/⅔ cup) white wine vinegar
150ml (5fl oz/⅔ cup) water
5g (⅛ oz/1 tsp) sea salt

Put the cauliflower in a large heatproof bowl. Bring the rest of the ingredients to the boil in a small saucepan, then carefully pour over the florets to cover. Leave for at least 1 hour before using. This will keep in an airtight container in the fridge for up to 2 weeks.

PICKLED SHALLOTS

Makes: 250ml (8½fl oz) jar

4 banana shallots
10g (¼oz/1¼ tsp) sea salt
20g (¾oz/1⅔ tbsp) caster (superfine) sugar
30ml (1fl oz/2 tbsp) white wine vinegar
300ml (10fl oz/1¼ cups) water
50ml (2fl oz/scant ¼ cup) extra virgin olive oil

Peel the shallots and slice into rings, keeping the root intact. Put the salt, sugar, vinegar and water into a saucepan and bring to the boil. As soon as it boils, add the shallots and simmer for just 2 minutes, then strain the shallots and discard the liquid. Toss the shallots in the olive oil. This will keep in an airtight container in the fridge for up to 2 weeks.

PICKLED BEETROOT (BEETS)

Makes: 150ml (5fl oz) jar

1 small white or red beetroot (beet))
25g (1oz/2 tbsp) caster (superfine) sugar
25ml (1fl oz/5 tsp) cider or white wine vinegar
50ml (2fl oz/scant ¼ cup) water
2.5g (scant ½ tsp) sea salt

If using a red beetroot (beet), line a chopping board with 4 layers of cling film (plastic wrap) and wear gloves to prevent staining. Peel the beetroot (beet) and cut into the largest cube you can. Cut into 2mm ($^1/_{16}$-inch) slices on a mandolin. Using a sharp knife cut each slice into 2mm ($^1/_{16}$-inch) strips. Then bunching the strips, cut them into 2mm ($^1/_{16}$-inch) cubes. Place the cubes in a small heatproof bowl.

Put the rest of the ingredients into a small saucepan and bring to the boil, then pour over the beetroot (beet). Leave for 2 hours then strain. This will keep in an airtight container in the fridge for up to 2 weeks.

« pickled shallots

pickled carrot »

« pickled pear

« pickled cauliflower

« sauerkraut

pickled beetroot (beets) »

« kimchi

PICKLED CARROTS

Makes: 250–500ml (8½–18fl oz) jar

3 large carrots, peeled and trimmed
25g (1oz/2 tbsp) caster (superfine) sugar
50ml (2fl oz/scant ¼ cup) white wine
50ml (2fl oz/scant ¼ cup) white wine vinegar
75ml (2¾fl oz/⅓ cup) water
3g (½ tsp) sea salt
50ml (2fl oz/scant ¼ cup) extra virgin olive oil
2g thyme sprigs (including stalks)
1 star anise

Using a mandolin, cut the carrots lengthways into ribbons to the thickness of cereal box card. Alternatively, cut the carrot into thin rounds using a sharp knife.

Bring the rest of the ingredients to the boil in a small saucepan, then remove from the heat and add the carrots. Stir well, then set aside to cool in the saucepan.

Once cold, transfer to a jar and store in the fridge for at least 4 hours before using. This will keep in the fridge for 2 weeks.

PICKLED KOHLRABI

Makes: 250ml (8½fl oz) jar

1 kohlrabi, skin removed
30g (1¼oz/2½ tbsp) caster (superfine) sugar
60ml (2¼fl oz/¼ cup) white wine vinegar
90ml (3¼fl oz/generous ⅓ cup) water

Cut the kohlrabi into even 5mm (¼-inch) cubes and put into a heatproof bowl.

Bring the rest of the ingredients to the boil in a small saucepan, then pour over the kohlrabi and leave to cool. Once cold, transfer to a storage jar and store in the fridge for at least 2 hours before using. This will keep for up to 2 weeks in the fridge.

PICKLED PEAR

Makes: 100ml (3½fl oz) jar

1 Williams pear
30g (1¼oz/2½ tbsp) caster (superfine) sugar
60ml (2¼fl oz/¼ cup) white wine vinegar
90ml (3¼fl oz/generous ⅓ cup) water
3g (½ tsp) sea salt

Peel the pear, cut into quarters, remove the core and cut into 7mm (⅓-inch) pieces.

Put the rest of the ingredients into a small saucepan and bring to the boil. Add the diced pear and cook for 20 seconds, then remove from the heat and allow to cool completely before using. This will keep in the fridge for 3 days.

PICKLED CABBAGE

Makes: 500ml–1-litre (17fl oz–1¾-pint) jar

1 small white cabbage
200g (7oz/1 cup) caster (superfine) sugar
400ml (13½fl oz/1⅔ cups) white wine vinegar
800ml (28fl oz/3⅓ cups) water
20g (¾oz/1¼ tbsp) sea salt
4 cloves
4g (2 tsp) caraway seeds

Cut the cabbage into quarters and remove the core. Slice very thinly using a mandolin and put into a large heatproof bowl.

Put the rest of the ingredients into a saucepan and bring to the boil, then immediately pour the liquid over the cabbage. Stir to ensure the cabbage is completely covered, then leave to pickle for at least 4 hours before using. This will keep in an airtight container in the fridge for up to 2 weeks.

SAUERKRAUT

Shop-bought sauerkraut bears almost no resemblance to the real thing. It has been mass produced and pasteurized, which almost completely defeats the point of it. Making it at home is really easy, and once it's made it will keep for months in the fridge.

Makes: 1-litre (1¾-pint) jar

1 large white cabbage, quartered and core removed
sea salt
pinch of caraway seeds (optional)

Sterilize a 1-litre (1¾-pint) glass jar by bringing a large saucepan of water to the boil and submerging the jar and lid in it. Boil for 10 minutes and then carefully remove. Allow to cool and dry.

Slice each cabbage quarter thinly crossways on a mandolin and place in a large, clean bowl. Weigh and calculate 2 per cent of the cabbage weight. Add that amount of salt (for 1kg (2¼lb) of cabbage add 20g (¾oz/1¼ tbsp) of salt).

Mix the cabbage and salt together and leave to stand for 10 minutes. Massage the mix for 2 minutes, then leave for a further 10 minutes. Keep repeating this until the water released covers the cabbage. Add a pinch or 2 of caraway seeds, if you wish, and mix in well. Transfer the cabbage to your prepared jar and then pour enough of the released liquid over the top to cover.

Cut a circle of baking parchment just bigger than the top of the jar and push this down inside the jar to keep the cabbage submerged under the liquid. Place the lid on the jar but do not fasten it. Place it somewhere with a warm, stable temperature (21°C/70°F) for 5 days. Check every day to make sure the water has not overflowed or disappeared.

After 5 days, take out the paper and taste the sauerkraut – it should taste pleasantly fermented. Return the paper to the top, firmly attach the lid and put into the fridge to store.

This will keep for at least 2 months in the fridge.

KIMCHI

Kimchi is sauerkraut's spicy cousin and takes four to five days to mature properly. There are as many recipes as there are people who make it, each with its own charms, but my version is very straightforward as I like to keep my flavours simple and clean.

Makes: 1-litre (1¾-pint) jar

1 small white cabbage, quartered and core removed
6 mild red chillies, cut in half lengthways, seeds discarded, sliced very thinly
4 spring onions (scallions), very finely sliced
2 carrots, peeled and coarsely grated
sea salt

Sterilize a 1-litre (1¾-pint) glass jar (see left). Follow all steps of the Sauerkraut method (left), adding the chillies, spring onions (scallions) and carrots to the sliced cabbage, and weighing the total mix to calculate the salt ratio.

After 5 days, try the kimchi. It should taste pleasantly fermented and a bit moreish. Return the paper to the top, firmly attach the lid and store in the fridge.

This will keep for at least 2 months in the fridge.

SALADS

I always used to cut fennel lengthways, to show off the shape of the bulb, but it was often a bit stringy as the fibres of the fennel run lengthways along the petals. At some point I realized that cutting fennel across, while not quite as visually satisfying, eliminated this problem. Food is firstly about how good it is to the mouth and only secondly to the eye, so now I cut my raw fennel across instead.

I learnt the technique used on the hazelnuts from Acorn's head chef Steven, and it is a great way to cook nuts, lifting this salad from good to great. It is, however, a lot of work for a scattering of nuts. Should you choose instead to pan-fry your hazelnuts in a little oil until golden, before sprinkling them with a touch of salt, no one would think any less of you, except possibly Steven.

Serves: 4

FENNEL & HAZELNUT SALAD

FOR THE DRESSING
30ml (1fl oz/2 tbsp) hazelnut oil
10ml (2 tsp) lemon juice
3g (½ tsp) sea salt

FOR THE SALAD
1 x quantity of candied hazelnuts
  (see page 114)
2 heads of red chicory (endive)
2 fennel bulbs
10g (¼oz/2⅔ tbsp) flat-leaf parsley
  leaves
10g (¼oz) chervil leaves

Prepare the candied hazelnuts (see page 114).

Mix the hazelnut oil, lemon juice and salt together to make the dressing. Separate out the chicory (endive) bulbs into leaves and cut any that are bigger than the length of your thumb into smaller pieces. Set to one side.

When ready to serve, prepare the fennel. Trim the bottom from the fennel to leave a flat base. Using a mandolin, slice the fennel bulb from the bottom into 1mm slices (very thin but with just enough thickness to retain a crunch). Put the chicory and sliced fennel together in a bowl and add the herb leaves. Mix dry to make sure they are well dispersed, then pour over the dressing and mix again well. Add the nuts, stir through and serve.

This salad goes very well with everyday bread (see page 214) or my green lentil & onion pâté (see page 72).

Good food cannot be rushed. The slow process of developing flavours and complexity is a pleasure in itself, one that is in danger of being lost in a world of 30-minute meals and quick-fix dinners. This salad takes several days to prepare well, but each gentle stage develops texture and flavour layers that simply using canned beans and roasted tomatoes cannot achieve. For me, good food is about using that ultimate and most precious of ingredients, time.

Serves: 4

CONFIT TOMATO SALAD
with white beans and black olives

FOR THE CONFIT TOMATOES
8 top-quality plum tomatoes
6g (1 tsp) sea salt
25ml (1fl oz/5 tsp) sherry vinegar (or red wine vinegar)
4g (⅛oz) thyme leaves
4g (⅛oz) sprigs of tarragon
4 whole cloves of garlic
750ml (26fl oz/3 cups) extra virgin olive oil

FOR THE WHITE BEANS
100g (3½oz/½ cup) dried cannellini beans
1 onion, cut into large chunks
3 sticks of celery, cut into large chunks
1 bay leaf
5g (⅛oz) sprigs of thyme
5g (⅛oz) sprigs of tarragon
10 black peppercorns
1 litre (1¾ pints/4 cups) water
5g (⅛oz/1 tsp) sea salt
10g (¼oz/1 tbsp) flat-leaf parsley leaves, finely chopped

TO SERVE
black olive tapenade (see page 36)
4 sliced black olives
handful of parsley leaves

You will need to prepare the confit tomatoes and soak the cannellini beans 1 day before serving. Remove the stem of each plum tomato, then cut a cross in the skin at the bottom. Blanch the tomatoes in boiling water until the skin starts to split, then shock in ice-cold water (see page 183). Peel off the skins, cut each tomato in half, discard the seeds and place in a large bowl. Add the salt, mix well and leave for 1 hour, then add the vinegar, herbs and garlic and stir well. Leave for at least 1 hour, but ideally overnight.

Put the dried beans in a large bowl and cover with cold water by at least 4cm (1½ inches). Soak for at least 6 hours and ideally overnight. Make the black olive tapenade (see page 36).

Preheat the oven to (fan) 100°C/120°C/240°F/gas mark ¼–½. Remove the tomatoes from the macerating juice (reserving the juice) and lay them face down in a baking tray (sheet) or casserole dish that is just big enough to fit them all in. Pour the olive oil over the tomatoes until they are just covered. Remove the garlic and herbs from the macerating liquid and put them in with the tomatoes. Bake the tomatoes for 30–40 minutes, until cooked but not breaking down. Transfer each tomato carefully to a plate and allow to cool, reserving the oil.

Meanwhile, drain and rinse the soaked beans and put them into a large saucepan with the onion, celery, bay leaf, thyme, tarragon and peppercorns. Add the measured water and gently bring to the boil. Half cover the saucepan with a lid and simmer gently, topping up the water if needed to keep the beans submerged, until they are tender but not broken up (this could take up to 2 hours). Top the water back up, add the salt and cook for 10 more minutes. Drain the beans and remove the onion, celery, herbs and peppercorns. Put the beans into a bowl and measure the macerating liquid from the tomatoes, then add it to the bowl with the beans. Add the same amount of reserved cooking oil and allow the beans to cool in the mix, ideally for several hours. When ready to serve, mix in the parsley.

Spoon the cannellini beans into the bottom of 4 low-sided starter bowls, with enough of the bean liquid dressing for the beans to sit in but not be covered. Arrange 4 tomato halves in each bowl, on top of the beans. Scatter with the sliced olives and parsley leaves and serve with the black olive tapenade. This is also delicious with crusty bread and a fresh green salad.

Pan-frying the cauliflower in this dish means that you don't need to heat a lot of oil as you do for the cauliflower and almond fritters (see page 174). It also means that the cauliflower fries unevenly, which in this case is a good thing, leading to charred tasty areas and softer sweeter ones.

Serves: 4

PAN-FRIED CAULIFLOWER SALAD
with a caper, pine nut and chilli dressing

FOR THE CAULIFLOWER
2 large cauliflowers
20g (¾oz/scant 3 tbsp) gram flour
5g (⅛oz/2 tsp) paprika
60ml (2¼fl oz/¼ cup) extra virgin
   olive oil, for frying

FOR THE DRESSING
40g (1½oz/¼ cup) small capers
   in salt
25g (1oz/3 tbsp) pine nuts
80ml (3fl oz/⅓ cup) extra virgin
   olive oil
2 cloves of garlic, puréed (see page
   145)
2 red chillies (not too hot), cut in
   half, deseeded and finely sliced
zest of 2 lemons
40ml (1½fl oz/8 tsp) lemon juice
20g (¾oz/⅓ cup) parsley leaves,
   finely chopped
20g (¾oz/¾ cup) mint leaves,
   finely sliced
4g (¾ tsp) sea salt

Put 4 litres (7 pints/16 cups) of water and 60g (2oz/3½ tbsp) of salt into a large saucepan and bring to the boil. Separate the cauliflower into florets and peel off any woody skin on the stem. Add the florets to the boiling water and simmer gently for 4–6 minutes until cooked but still al dente (a knife will just pass through the stem). Shock in ice-cold water (see page 183), then drain and pat dry.

Preheat the oven to (fan) 160°C/180°C/350°F/gas mark 4.

Make the dressing. Place the capers in a small bowl and cover with cold water. Drain and re-cover with water, then leave to soak for 1 hour. Put the pine nuts on a small baking tray (sheet) and bake in the oven for 5 minutes. Leave to cool slightly, then crush gently using a pestle and mortar, so they are just broken with some whole pieces. Remove the capers from the water (leaving the salt) and dry on kitchen (paper) towel.

Heat the olive oil in a small saucepan and add the capers. Fry gently until they begin to go crispy, then add the garlic and fry for 30 seconds. Remove from the heat, stir in the chillies and pine nuts and allow to cool. Add the lemon zest and juice, parsley, mint and salt to the saucepan. Mix well.

Mix the gram flour and paprika together in a small bowl. Lightly sprinkle it over the cauliflower florets, making sure there is a light coating with no lumps, then rub it on. Turn the cauliflower over and do the same on the other side. Heat the olive oil in a large, wide-based frying pan (skillet), place the cauliflower in the pan and fry until a deep golden brown. Turn over and repeat on the other side. You may need to cook it in batches, adding more oil if necessary, keeping the cooked cauliflower warm.

Serve the cauliflower with the dressing drizzled generously over the top.

Cylindra beetroots (beets) are a long, dark red variety with a flavour profile identical to the round dark red varieties. Their main advantage is they are an even width down most of their length, so when you slice them all of your slices are the same size. If you can only find the round variety then cut them into wedges as this is a better way of ensuring they cook at the same speed.

Serves: 4

ROASTED CYLINDRA BEETROOT (BEETS)
with crushed blackberry dressing and pistachio purée

FOR THE ROASTED BEETROOT (BEETS)
2 large cylindra beetroot (beets)
10g (¼oz) sprigs of thyme
1g (a pinch) dried lavender
5g (⅛oz/1 tsp) sea salt
50ml (2fl oz/scant ¼ cup) water
25ml (1fl oz/5 tsp) extra virgin olive oil

FOR THE DRESSING
40ml (1½fl oz/8 tsp) thyme oil (see page 220)
100g (3½oz/⅔ cup) blackberries, quartered
5ml (1 tsp) red wine vinegar
3g (⅔ tsp) caster (superfine) sugar
pinch of sea salt

FOR THE PURÉE
100g (3½oz/¾ cup) Iranian pistachios
100ml (3½fl oz/scant ½ cup) extra virgin olive oil
150ml (5fl oz/⅔ cup) water
1 clove of garlic
sea salt
pinch of cayenne pepper

FOR THE GARNISH
10g (¼oz/generous 1 tbsp) Iranian pistachios, cut into large chunks
2 sprigs of thyme, leaves picked
20 small red mustard frill leaves

You need to make the thyme oil at least a day, and preferably up to 2 weeks, in advance (see page 220).

Preheat the oven to (fan) 140°C/160°C/310°F/gas mark 2½. Place a 45cm (18-inch) strip of foil over a deep baking tray (sheet) and cover with a 45cm (18-inch) strip of baking parchment, forming a well in the middle. Put the beetroot (beets) and the rest of the beetroot (beet) ingredients into the well and mix together. Fold the tin foil/paper in half and roll up the edges to form a sealed parcel. Bake for 1–2 hours.

About 30 minutes before the beetroot (beets) are cooked, make the blackberry dressing. Put the blackberries in a small bowl and add the vinegar, sugar and salt. Gently crush the blackberries with the back of a fork to break them up but do not reduce them to a purée. Leave to macerate for 20 minutes, then stir in the thyme oil and set aside.

Next make the pistachio purée. Blend the pistachios, olive oil, water and garlic in a blender until silky smooth. Season with salt and a pinch of cayenne pepper (see page 13). Set aside.

After 1–2 hours of cooking test the beetroot (beets) – they should be meltingly soft. If not ready, cook for a little longer then re-test. When ready, allow to cool a little and then rub the skin from the beetroot. Cut them into 1cm (½-inch) slices.

Place 2 tablespoons of pistachio purée on each of 4 starter-sized plates and allow it to run out to make a round pool. Place 2–3 slices of the warm beetroot (beets) across each other next to the purée, and scoop some of the blackberry dressing over the top. Scatter with the chopped pistachios and thyme leaves. Toss the mustard frill leaves in the remaining liquid from the blackberries and arrange on the plates. Serve warm.

Figs have a wonderful, complex sweetness and are perfect partners to red wine, bitter leaves and, surprisingly, curry. This salad plays with a few different flavour partners and, as is often the case with flavours that revolve around a central ingredient, finds a harmony and balance between them. Enjoy this salad with crusty bread and a glass of heavy red wine.

Serves: 4

RED WINE POACHED FIGS
with candied curried pecans and pickled shallots

FOR THE POACHED FIGS
450ml (16fl oz/scant 2 cups)
    red wine
40g (1½oz/¼ cup) brown sugar
2 cloves
1 bay leaf
6 sprigs of thyme
6g (⅛oz/1 tsp) sea salt
10 figs

FOR THE SALAD
curried candied pecans (see
    page 115)
pickled shallots (see page 96)
fig chutney (see page 36)
fresh winter salad leaves, such
    as watercress and red chicory
    (endive)
2 fresh figs, thinly sliced

Make the curried candied pecans (see page 115), pickled shallots (see page 96) and fig chutney (see page 36).

Preheat the oven to (fan) 160°C/180°C/350°F/gas mark 4. Put all the poaching ingredients, except the figs, into a small saucepan and bring to the boil.

Cut the figs in half lengthways and place cut side down on a deep baking tray (sheet). Pour the boiling wine over them, then place in the oven. Cook for 20–30 minutes, shaking gently every 10 minutes to make sure they remain moist. Check after 20 minutes – they should have softened a little but still hold their shape. When cooked, remove from the oven and allow to cool.

Pour the wine from the figs back into the saucepan and simmer gently until it reduces to a syrup. Pour the red wine reduction back over the figs.

Arrange a handful of salad leaves and the fresh fig slices on each plate. Split the poached fig halves between each plate and drizzle the red wine reduction over the top. Scatter several curried candied pecans on each plate and add rounds of pickled shallot. Put a scoop of fig chutney on the side and serve with crusty bread if you wish.

| GARNISHES |

MIXED TOASTED SEEDS

This makes enough for about 10 meals, although you can easily just eat them all without really meaning to straight from the oven – they're very moreish.

Makes: 1 small jar

20g (¾oz/2½ tbsp) sunflower seeds
5g (⅛oz/½ tbsp) poppy seeds
10g (¼oz/4 tsp) sesame seeds
10g (¼oz/1 tbsp) flax seeds
10g (¼oz/4 tsp) hemp seeds
½ tsp extra virgin olive oil
1g (scant ¼ tsp) sea salt, finely ground

Preheat the oven to (fan) 160°C/180°C/350°F/gas mark 4. Mix all the seeds together with the oil on a baking tray (sheet) and roast for 5 minutes until just golden. Sprinkle with the salt and allow to cool.

These can be kept in an airtight container for up to 2 weeks.

ROASTED CHICKPEAS (GARBANZO BEANS)

If you use a lot of aquafaba (see page 36), then you'll end up with a lot of chickpeas (garbanzo beans). Roasting them makes them a great texture for salads or soups, and they will keep for longer.

Makes: 1 small jar

50g (1¾oz/⅓ cup) chickpeas (garbanzo beans)
10ml (2 tsp) extra virgin olive oil
0.5g (¼ tsp) fennel seeds
large pinch of sea salt

Preheat the oven to (fan) 160°C/180°C/350°F/gas mark 4.

Mix all the ingredients together and put onto a small baking tray (sheet). Bake in the oven for 15 minutes until crisp and golden, mixing every 5 minutes.

Remove from the oven and drain on kitchen (paper) towel. Leave to cool, then place on a board and crush with the side of a large knife.

This will keep for up to 3 days in an airtight container.

SEEDED FREEKEH

Freekeh is a little like couscous, but made from toasted wheat. Using toasted seeds in this mix helps to emphasize its nutty character and makes it deliciously moreish.

Serves: 4

300g (10½oz/2 cups) freekeh
10ml (2 tsp) extra virgin olive oil
60g (2oz/scant ½ cup) sunflower seeds
30g (1¼oz/scant ¼ cup) pumpkin seeds
10g (¼oz/4 tsp) sesame seeds

Bring 3 litres (5¼ pints/12½ cups) of water and 30g (1¼oz/1¾ tbsp) of salt to the boil in a large saucepan. Add the freekeh and boil for 10–15 minutes until soft then drain.

Put the oil into a large frying pan (skillet) and add the sunflower seeds and pumpkin seeds. Heat the pan and gently fry the seeds until they pop and become golden then add the sesame seeds and stir. Add the cooked freekeh and stir to mix the seeds through the freekeh.

This is best eaten straight away.

PISTACHIO DUKKAH

Dukkah is a blend of nuts and spices used as a garnish in the Middle East. This uses pistachios, because they have a more buttery texture than most nuts.

Makes: 1 small jar

10g (¼oz/1¾ tbsp) coriander seeds
2.5g (1¼ tsp) cumin seeds
5g (⅛oz/1 tsp) sea salt
15g (½oz/2 tbsp) sesame seeds
50g (1¾oz/⅓ cup) Iranian pistachios

Preheat the oven to (fan) 160°C/180°C/350°F/gas mark 4. Toast the coriander seeds and cumin seeds together in a hot frying pan (skillet) until fragrant. Using a pestle and mortar, grind the coriander seeds, cumin seeds and salt to a coarse sandy texture. Transfer to a bowl.

On 2 baking trays (sheets) roast the sesame seeds and pistachios separately in the oven for 4 minutes, then leave to cool. Use the pestle and mortar to grind the sesame seeds to break them up, then transfer to the bowl with the spices. Crush the pistachios using the pestle and mortar to form crumbs. Add to the spices in the bowl and mix to combine.

This will keep for up to 1 month in an airtight container.

BLACK OLIVE CRUMBS

Something wonderful happens when you dry olives out – they become salty, intense and delicious. These black olive crumbs are great with any dish that needs a salty bitter edge.

Makes: 2 tablespoons

50g (1¾oz/⅓ cup) good-quality pitted black kalamata olives

Ideally use a dehydrator set to 45°C/113°F or preheat the oven to its lowest setting.

Spread the olives out on a dehydrator tray and dehydrate for 6 hours or until very dry and crispy. If using the oven, spread on a baking tray (sheet) and check every hour, turning them over, and cook for 6 hours. Chop into crumbs.

This will keep in an airtight container for up to 2 weeks.

CANDIED FENNEL SEEDS

These are great sprinkled over desserts, but are equally good as a little spattering of interest over salads or soups. If you are lucky enough to grow fennel, let a few bulbs run to seed and harvest them for the freshest, cleanest taste you can imagine.

Makes: 80g (3oz)

60g (2oz/⅓ cup) caster (superfine) sugar
30ml (1fl oz/2 tbsp) water
60g (2oz/⅔ cup) fennel seeds

Put the sugar and water in a small, heavy-based saucepan and heat to 137°C/278°F. Remove from the heat and add the fennel seeds. Stir hard until the sugar crystallizes and the fennel seeds separate from each other.

These will keep in an airtight container for up to 3 months.

SMOKED NUTS

Smoke and nuts is a fantastic modern flavour. Use these to bring a wonderful interest to any plate.

Makes: 100g (3½oz)

100g (3½oz/¾ cup) blanched hazelnuts, almonds
  or cashew nuts

Put 1 tablespoon of hickory chips into a stove-top smoker. Line the top grate with foil to prevent the nuts from escaping and follow the manufacturer's instructions.

Smoke the nuts until they have a pronounced smoky flavour. Remove from the smoker and leave to cool.

These will keep for 2 weeks in an airtight container.

CANDIED HAZELNUTS OR ALMONDS

This is a great way of preparing nuts to add not only a nutty edge but also a little sweetness to a dish.

Makes: 100g (3½ oz)

100g (3½oz/½ cup) caster (superfine) sugar
100ml (3½fl oz/scant ½ cup) water
50g (1¾oz/⅓ cup) blanched hazelnuts or almonds
neutral oil, for deep-fat frying

Prepare your deep-fat fryer (see page 24).

Put all the ingredients into a small saucepan and bring to the boil. Simmer gently until the water reaches 110°C/230°F and then strain the nuts from the liquid.

Add the nuts to the deep-fat fryer and fry for about 2 minutes until a light golden colour. Remove the nuts from the oil and transfer to a baking tray (sheet) or plate (do not line it with kitchen (paper) towel as the nuts will stick). Leave to cool.

These will keep in an airtight container for up to 1 month.

IMPROVISED SMOKER

If you don't have a stove-top smoker, you can improvise using a steamer basket. Put a piece of foil on the base of the steamer saucepan to prevent the chips from discolouring it. Put the smoking chips on to the foil and heat the saucepan on a medium–high heat until the chips burn. (If they don't burn, then use a blowtorch, lighter or match.) Once they are burning well, put on the steamer basket (containing the ingredients intended to smoke) and then put on the lid. Turn down the heat to medium and leave for 10–15 minutes until the desired level of smokiness is achieved.

CURRIED CANDIED PECANS

These are one of my favourite things in the world. I struggle to stop eating them, and only knowing the price of pecans slows me down.

Makes: 120g (4¼oz)

100g (3½oz/scant 1 cup) pecan nuts
10g (¼oz/1⅔ tbsp) mild Madras curry powder
2g (⅓ tsp) sea salt
100g (3½oz/½ cup) caster (superfine) sugar
30ml (1fl oz/2 tbsp) water

Preheat the oven to (fan) 160°C/180°C/350°F/gas mark 4. Put the pecan nuts on a baking tray (sheet) and roast for 8 minutes, then set aside to cool.

Mix the curry powder and salt with the pecans in a small bowl.

Put the sugar in a small, heavy-based saucepan with the water and heat gently until it reaches 137°C/278°F. Remove immediately from the heat and add the pecans, stirring very hard until the sugar crystallizes and the pecans separate from each other. Leave to cool.

These will keep for 3 months in an airtight container.

CURRIED POPCORN

If you're cooking with sweetcorn and you need to add a bit of texture, it seems silly not to use popcorn. This version adds curry flavours, but fresh rosemary, chilli and black pepper are also fantastic with popcorn.

Makes: 2 cups

2g (1 tsp) mild Madras curry powder
1g (scant ¼ tsp) sea salt
10ml (2 tsp) rapeseed oil
30g (1¼oz/⅛ cup) popcorn kernels

Using a pestle and mortar, grind the curry powder and salt to a powder.

Put the oil into a heavy-based lidded saucepan along with 2 popcorn kernels. Heat the oil with the lid on until the 2 kernels pop, then remove them and add the remaining kernels. Stir to coat them all in oil. Put the lid on and shake the saucepan constantly. The kernels should begin to pop frantically.

Once the popping slows to every 3 seconds, remove the saucepan from the heat and sprinkle in your curry powder mix.

This will keep for 3 days in an airtight container.

A NOTE ON CURRY POWDER

As a general rule I hate using pre-made anything, preferring the fresh flavour, control and craftman's satisfaction you get from creating everything from scratch. However, the one thing that has defeated me is Madras curry powder – I never seem to be able to recreate the magical harmony of spices you get from a good-quality shop-bought mix. Each brand has its own blend of spices, but any good-quality brand should deliver the necessary complexity. Just make sure it is a mild mix, as anything spicy will throw a whole new element into the mix.

CABBAGE POWDER

Sometimes you want to add a deep, cooked cabbage note to a dish without the complication or texture of cooked leaves. This powder achieves that and also adds a great visual texture to a plate. As you use it sparingly, this will make enough for about 20 servings.

Makes: 1–2 tbsp

200g (7oz) dark green spring green or cabbage leaves

Ideally use a dehydrator set to 45°C/113°F, or preheat the oven to its lowest setting.

Put 4 litres (7 pints/16 cups) of water and 40g (1½oz/2½ tbsp) of salt into a large saucepan and bring to the boil. Blanch the cabbage leaves for 1 minute and shock in ice-cold water (see page 183).

Spread the cabbage out on a dehydrator tray and dehydrate for 8 hours or until very dry and crispy. If using the oven, spread out on a baking tray (sheet) and cook for 6–8 hours.

Using a spice grinder or pestle and mortar, grind the dried leaves to a fine powder. This will keep in a jar for 2 weeks.

ONION POWDER

You can buy onion powder, but it is never as fresh and sweet as when you make it yourself.

Makes: 100g (3½oz)

4 brown-skinned onions, peeled and sliced

Ideally use a dehydrator set to 45°C/113°F, or preheat the oven to its lowest setting.

Spread the onion slices out on a dehydrator tray and dehydrate for 4 hours until dry and crispy, with a little colour. If using the oven, spread out on a baking tray (sheet) and cook for 6–8 hours.

Using a pestle and mortar grind the onions into a fine powder. This will keep in an airtight container for up to 2 months.

PORCINI POWDER

This will make a lot of powder, but you will find that it is easier to blend large quantities and there are numerous uses for it once you have it to hand. If you are lucky enough to have an electric coffee grinder then blend what you need, when you need it, to guarantee a fresh bright flavour.

Makes: 90g (3oz)

100g (3½oz) dried porcini mushrooms

Put the porcinis into a blender or spice grinder and blend to a fine powder.

This will keep in a sealed jar for months.

ORANGE ZEST POWDER

This adds citrus notes, a splash of colour and interest to any dish so it's well worth having a jar in your cupboard. Although this only makes a couple of tablespoons that is enough for about 20 servings.

Makes: 1–2 tablespoons

4 organic, unwaxed oranges

Ideally use a dehydrator set to 45°C/113°F, or preheat the oven to its lowest setting.

Peel the zest from the orange in strips, avoiding as much of the white pith as you can. Put the strips onto a dehydrator tray and dehydrate for 8 hours or until completely dry and brittle. If using the oven, place on a baking tray (sheet) and dry out for 2 hours, then check.

Using a pestle and mortar, grind the dried strips into a fine powder.

This will keep for 2 weeks in an airtight container.

ORANGE ZAATAR MIX

Zaatar traditionally uses sumac powder to bring acidity and colour to the mix. Substituting this for orange zest powder (see left) tones down the acidity, replacing it with an astringency and brings more citrus notes, making it great for adding aromas to a dish without upsetting the acidity balance. This makes enough for four servings.

Makes: 2 tablespoons

15g (½oz/2 tbsp) sesame seeds
5g (⅛oz/2½ tsp) cumin seeds
3g (½ tbsp) fennel seeds
5g (⅛oz) orange zest powder (see left)

Preheat the oven to (fan) 160°C/180°C/350°F/gas mark 4. Put the sesame seeds on a small baking tray (sheet) and toast in the oven for 5 minutes.

Mix the cumin and fennel seeds together, place on a small baking tray (sheet), and toast in the oven for 5 minutes. Leave to cool, then grind the cumin and fennel seeds to a coarse sand texture using a pestle and mortar.

Mix all the ingredients together. This will keep for 2 weeks in an airtight container.

MAINS

Cavatelli means 'little hollow' in Italian and you should keep this in mind when making it. The technique for making it is very similar to rolling gnocchi (see page 136), but whereas gnocchi are dumplings, cavatelli should have a little air in the middle – you achieve this by squashing them down a little more firmly when rolling them. Don't stress too much about it to begin with, whatever you make will be edible, but aim for little hollows.

Serves: 4

CAVATELLI
with asparagus and pine nut sauce

25ml (1fl oz/5 tsp) light oil (such as rapeseed)
20 asparagus spears, woody bases snapped off and discarded
sea salt

FOR THE CAVATELLI
405g (14⅓oz/2⅓ cups) semolina, plus extra for dusting
135g (4¾oz/1 cup) type 00 flour
240g (8½oz) water

FOR THE PINE NUT SAUCE
15ml (1 tbsp) extra virgin olive oil
3 cloves of garlic, minced
100g (3½oz) pine nut butter (see page 219)
100g (3½oz) baby spinach
25ml (1fl oz/5 tsp) truffle oil

TO SERVE
freshly ground black pepper
finely grated lemon zest

To make the cavatelli dough, put the semolina, 00 flour and water into a mixing bowl and mix into a rough dough. Cover the dough with either the upturned bowl or cling film (plastic wrap) and leave it for 15 minutes to relax. After it is rested, knead lightly on a clean work surface until smooth and silky. This should happen fairly quickly. Once smooth, form into a ball, wrap in cling film (plastic wrap) to prevent a skin from forming and allow to rest for at least 30 minutes – ideally 2 hours in the fridge – before using. You can store the dough in the fridge for up to 3 days. Be warned though, it will soften and become gummy the longer you keep it. When ready to make the pasta, unwrap the dough and shape it according to the method on page 125.

Use a peeler to carefully remove any woody or stringy skin near the base of the trimmed asparagus spears and trim into pieces slightly longer than the pasta pieces you have made.

Heat the light oil in a large frying pan (skillet) over a high heat until very hot. Add the asparagus spears, sprinkle with a little salt and fry them hard until they take on a dark fried colour and are just becoming soft up by the tip. They will continue to soften off the heat as you prepare the sauce and pasta so err on the side of slightly underdone. Remove from the pan, transfer to a baking tray (sheet) and keep somewhere warm while you cook the pasta and sauce. (Cook the pasta according to the method on page 125.)

While the pasta cooks, heat the extra virgin olive oil and garlic gently in a clean sauté pan until the garlic softens, then add a splash of the pasta cooking water with a ladle. Add the pine nut butter and enough additional pasta cooking water to create a thin cream-like consistency. Add the spinach leaves and stir to wilt.

When the pasta floats to the surface allow it to cook for 2 minutes more and then remove one to test for doneness: it should be firm but cooked through (beware a raw centre). When cooked, remove the pasta with a spider or slotted spoon and place straight into the prepared pine nut sauce. Toss the pasta gently in the sauce and heat until it is the perfect thickness (it should coat the back of a tablespoon), then remove from the heat, add the truffle oil and stir it through.

Spoon the mix onto 4 warmed, rimmed plates or large pasta bowls and split the pasta and sauce among them. Place the asparagus artfully on top and finish with a crack of black pepper and a little finely grated lemon zest.

This dish is all about the fresh green colour and flavour – the quality of your ingredients and the craft of your pasta work should have the space to sing. Use the freshest beans you can find, the most vibrant basil, and take your time making the perfect trofie. Use this recipe as a guide to how many beans you will need (include the same amount of beans as trofie), just use an abundance of different kinds to make this a true celebration of the season.

Serves: 4

SPINACH TROFIE
with summer beans and pesto

FOR THE TROFIE
125g (4½oz/4 cups) spinach
75ml (2¾fl oz/⅓ cup) water
300g (10½oz/1¾ cups) fine yellow
  semolina, plus extra to dust
15ml (1 tbsp) extra virgin olive oil

FOR THE BEANS
100g (3½oz) fine green (string)
  beans
100g (3½oz) podded broad (fava)
  beans
100g (3½oz) runner beans
100g (3½oz) fine asparagus

FOR THE PESTO SAUCE
150g (5½oz) pesto (see page 38)
50ml (2fl oz/scant ¼ cup) water
50ml (2fl oz/scant ¼ cup) extra
  virgin olive oil

FOR THE GARNISH
20g (¾oz/2½ tbsp) pine nuts
10g (¼oz/⅓ cup) small basil leaves
  (or large leaves, shredded)
black pepper
extra virgin olive oil

First make the pesto (see page 38). Next make the spinach trofie. Blanch the spinach for 30 seconds, until wilted and a vibrant green, then shock in ice-cold water (see page 183). Once cold, collect it into a ball, squeezing out all the water. Roughly chop the ball and place in a blender. Add the measured water and blend to a very smooth purée, with no flecks of green in it.

Measure 140g (5oz) of the spinach purée into a large bowl and add the semolina and olive oil. Using a spoon, bring the pasta mix together to form a rough dough, then transfer to a clean, dry work surface. Knead the dough for about 8 minutes, until smooth and supple. Wrap in cling film (plastic wrap) and put in the fridge for 30 minutes to rest, and ideally for longer as it will get firmer and easier to work with. It will keep for up to 3 days in the fridge, just remove from the fridge 30 minutes before using.

Preheat the oven to (fan) 160°C/180°C/350°F/gas mark 4. Put the pine nuts for the garnish on a small baking tray (sheet) and toast in the oven for 4 minutes. Remove and allow to cool.

Make the spinach trofie (see Shaping Trofie, page 125).

Prepare each type of bean and the asparagus, removing any woody stalks or strings. Blanch the beans and asparagus until al dente (between 30 seconds and 2 minutes depending on the bean), one type of bean at a time to make sure each type is perfectly cooked, then shock in ice-cold water (see page 183). You want them to have a fresh crunch. Cook the trofie (see cooking pasta, page 125).

Put the water and olive oil for the pesto sauce into a large saucepan and bring to the boil. Add the trofie and heat for 30 seconds. Add the beans and heat until everything is just hot. Add the pesto and stir so that it coats everything.

Split the mix between 4 pasta bowls or plates and scatter with the toasted pine nuts, basil, a generous twist of black pepper and a drizzle of olive oil. Serve hot.

| MAKING PASTA |

ROLLING OUT PASTA USING A PASTA MACHINE

Knead the made pasta briefly, then form it into a ball and divide into 4 to 6 pieces. Form the first piece into a rough rectangle then, using a rolling pin, roll into a rectangle about 1cm (½ inch) narrower than the width of your pasta machine.

Set the machine to its widest setting and feed the pasta through. Fold it in half lengthways and feed it back through, it should now be a neat rectangle the same width as the machine.

Reduce the machine thickness by one setting and feed the pasta through again. Continue this process, dusting it with semolina when necessary, until you reach the thickness you want. Repeat with the rest of the pieces of dough.

MAKING PAPPARDELLE

Roll out the pasta using a pasta machine (see above) until the third to last thickness on the machine.

Dust your work surface with semolina and lay the pasta out. Dust well with semolina. Using a fluted pasta roller (or knife) cut the pasta into 2.5cm (1-inch) wide strips across the width of the pasta.

SHAPING TORTELLINI

Roll out the pasta using a pasta machine (see left) until the second to last thickness on the machine.

Dust your work surface with semolina and lay the pasta out. Using a cutter the same size as the width of your pasta sheet (up to 15cm/6 inches), cut as many rounds from it as you can.

Line a baking tray (sheet) with cling film (plastic wrap) and lightly oil it. Mix together 50g (1¾oz/generous ⅓ cup) of plain (all-purpose) flour and 100ml (3½fl oz/scant ½ cup) of water into a paste in a small bowl and set aside.

Pipe or spoon 1 small tablespoon of the filling into the centre of each round. Getting the right amount of filling is critical – too little and the pasta is disappointingly empty; too much, and it will burst open.

Using your finger, spread the flour and water mix onto one half of each pasta round to act as a glue and then fold each round over into a half-moon shape, encapsulating the filling in a neat bulge in the middle.

Using the soft pad of your thumb or finger, carefully but firmly press the pasta down to stick, pushing all the air out of the middle as you do so. You are trying to do 3 things: shape the filling into a neat bubble surrounded by pasta, eliminate any air pockets from the centre, and stick the 2 halves of pasta together. Once you have sealed all the parcels, take the cutter you used earlier and, using a rolling motion, trim the rough edge from your half-moon shape.

Now the tricky part. Dab one corner of the moon liberally with the flour paste and then, using your thumb to form a little crease in the filling bubble, fold both corners toward the middle sticking one to the other and pressing firmly.

Place each finished tortellini on the oiled tray, cover with cling film (plastic wrap) and pop in the fridge for up to 8 hours until needed.

SHAPING CAVATELLI

(See page 120)

Lightly dust your work surface with semolina. Cut the pasta dough into 8 equal pieces. Roll each piece into a sausage 7mm (⅓ inch) thick and cut each sausage into 1.5cm (½-inch) lengths.

Using a pasta board, butter pat or fork take each piece of dough and, using your thumb, in one smooth motion press and roll the dough down the board to flatten it and roll it into a shell-like shape, a little like gnocchi (see page 136). It may take a few attempts to get this right, but persevere as it will be worth it.

SHAPING TROFIE

(See page 123)

Line a baking tray (sheet) with baking parchment and dust with a little semolina. Cut the pasta into 8 equal pieces and roll out each piece into a 5mm (¼-inch) thick sausage.

Cut the sausage into 1cm (½-inch) lengths. Roll each piece into a long, torpedo shape between the palms of your hand.

Set a blunt knife at a 45 degree angle in your hand and set this at 45 degrees to the pasta. Put the knife on the right-hand end of the pasta and pull the knife towards you, pulling the pasta with it and drawing it across to twist the pasta (this is easier than it sounds).

Develop a rhythm and work through the pile as quickly as you can. Dust lightly with semolina and transfer to the prepared baking tray (sheet).

COOKING PASTA

Fill a large saucepan with 6 litres (10 pints/25 cups) of water, add 60g (2oz/3½ tbsp) of salt and bring to the boil.

Using a dough knife or spatula, scoop the pasta into the boiling water. If the water stops boiling, don't add more pasta, just finish the batch already cooking before adding more.

When the pasta floats to the surface allow it to cook for 2 minutes for cavatelli, 1–2 minures for trofie and 5 seconds for pappardelle until al dente. Remove one to test – it should be firm but cooked through. When cooked, remove the pasta with a spider or slotted spoon.

If you don't want to go to the effort of making all the components, then just make the pasta and the courgette (zucchini) mix and combine them in a saucepan before serving. It's not as pretty, but it is just as tasty.

Serves: 4

FENNEL SEED PAPPARDELLE

with courgettes (zucchini), chickpeas (garbanzo beans), basil and lemon

FOR THE PAPPARDELLE

1.5g (¾ tsp) fennel seeds
160ml (5½fl oz/⅔ cup) boiling water
400g (xxoz/x cups) fine semolina, plus extra to dust
15ml (1 tbsp) extra virgin olive oil, plus extra to drizzle

FOR THE GRIDDLED COURGETTES (ZUCCHINI)

2 large courgettes (zucchini)
sea salt
extra virgin olive oil

FOR THE COURGETTE (ZUCCHINI) MIX

3 large courgettes (zucchini)
80g (2¾oz/½ cup) canned chickpeas (garbanzo beans), drained and rinsed
3g (½ tsp) sea salt
50ml (2fl oz/scant ¼ cup) water
75ml (2¾fl oz/⅓ cup) extra virgin olive oil
1 dried chilli
1 clove of garlic, puréed (see page 145)
zest of ½ lemon
25ml (1fl oz/5 tsp) lemon juice
20g (¾oz/generous ¾ cup) basil leaves, shredded

FOR THE GARNISH

roasted chickpeas (garbanzo beans) (see page 112)
1 lemon
10g (¼oz/ ⅓ cup) basil leaves
chilli flakes (crushed chilli)

Make the roasted chickpea (garbanzo bean) garnish (see page 112). To make the pappardelle, grind the fennel seeds to a fine powder using a pestle and mortar. Add the boiling water and leave to infuse for 20 minutes. Put the semolina into a large bowl, add the olive oil and measure in the fennel water, first weighing it and making it up to 160g (5¾oz) with cold water. Using a spoon, bring the pasta mix together to form a rough dough, then transfer to a clean, dry work surface. Knead the dough for about 8 minutes, until smooth and supple. Wrap in cling film (plastic wrap) and put in the fridge for 30 minutes, then make the pasta (see making pappardelle, page 124).

Cut the courgettes (zucchini) for the griddled courgettes (zucchini) lengthways into thin strips (about 3mm/⅛ inch) on a mandolin. Weigh, add 1 per cent of their weight in salt, mix well and leave for 30 minutes. Meanwhile, make the courgette (zucchini) mix. Put 4 litres (7 pints/16 cups) of water into a large saucepan with 40g (1½oz/ 2½ tbsp) of salt and bring to the boil. Add the whole courgettes (zucchini) and cook for 10–15 minutes, until soft, then remove to a colander to cool. Put the chickpeas (garbanzo beans), salt, water, 50ml (2fl oz/scant ¼ cup) of olive oil and the dried chilli into a small saucepan and cook gently until the water has just evaporated. Add the garlic, then remove from the heat and set aside.

When the boiled courgettes (zucchini) are cool, cut off and discard the top and bottom and cut into 7mm (⅓ inch) dice. Return to the colander, then using a small plate push down to remove any liquid. Transfer the courgette (zucchini) to a large bowl, and add the hot chickpea (garbanzo bean) mix, lemon zest, lemon juice, basil and the rest of the olive oil. Stir well.

Rinse the courgette (zucchini) slices and dry with kitchen (paper) towel. Heat a griddle pan until very hot and brush the slices with oil. Char, in batches if necessary, on the griddle pan until black ridges appear on one side. Turn over and repeat on the other side. Once cooked, roll up, transfer to a bowl and add a drizzle of olive oil.

Cook the pappardelle in 2 batches (see cooking pasta, page 125). Cook one batch, then put them on a tray lined with non-stick baking parchment. Drizzle with a little olive oil and flatten them out to prevent them sticking. Cover lightly with a clean tea towel and repeat with the rest. Arrange a quarter of the pappardelle on each of 4 large plates. Arrange spoonfuls of the courgette (zucchini) mix and the rolled griddled courgette around the plate and over the pappardelle. Grate a little lemon zest over and sprinkle whole and shredded basil, chilli flakes (crushed chilli) and roasted chickpea (garbanzo) crumble over the top, then serve.

This dish has some big flavours, but the balance is delicate and refined. To make this really well you must remember a few basic principles: the most important of which is that your filling must be firm. If your filling is wet, it will make the tortellini hard to shape and they will go soggy and split. I have suggested adding a little water to the potato mix, but I do so with extreme caution, as I would rather have a coarse filling than a wet mix. Your pasta must also be delicate, and you need to make the filling a day in advance, which means you need to soak the walnuts two days in advance of eating.

Serves: 4

WALNUT TORTELLINI
with a red wine mushroom reduction

FOR THE WALNUT FILLING
200g (7oz/2 cups) walnuts
400g (14oz) whole new potatoes, skin on
30ml (1 fl oz/2 tbsp) walnut oil
50ml (2fl oz/scant ¼ cup) water (if needed)
2.5g (1 tbsp) chopped dill
tiny pinch of cayenne pepper

FOR THE TORTELLINI
0.3g (scant ½ tsp) saffron
175ml (6fl oz/¾ cup) boiling water
400g (14oz/2⅓ cups) fine semolina, plus extra to dust
15ml (1 tbsp) extra virgin olive oil

FOR THE RED WINE REDUCTION
1 litre (1¾ pints/4 cups) mushroom stock (see page 63)
200ml (7fl oz/generous ¾ cup) red wine
1 bay leaf

Put the walnuts in a small bowl and cover with cold water by at least 2cm (¾ inch). Put into the fridge for at least 8 hours or overnight. Prepare the cavolo nero crisps (see page 26) and mushroom stock (see page 63).

Put the potatoes for the filling into a small saucepan with 1 litre (1¾ pints/4 cups) of water and 10g (¼oz/1¾ tsp) of salt and gently bring to the boil, covered with a lid. Simmer gently until the potatoes are soft, then drain.

While the potatoes are still hot, drain and rinse the walnuts. Put the walnuts into a blender and blend until as fine as possible. Transfer the walnuts to a large bowl and add the warm potatoes (with their skins on) and the walnut oil. Mash well, then return to the blender and process until a smooth, creamy texture, adding a little water if necessary. Be careful though, you need a firm mix. When smooth, transfer to a bowl and stir in the dill. Add a tiny pinch of cayenne pepper and check and adjust the seasoning (see page 13). Transfer to a piping bag or small container and put in the fridge for at least 4 hours to firm up.

Make the pasta. Grind the saffron to a fine powder using a pestle and mortar, then add the boiling water and leave to infuse for 20 minutes. Once the saffron is ready, put the semolina into a large bowl, add the olive oil and measure in the saffron water, making it back up to 175ml (6fl oz/¾ cup) with cold water. Using a spoon, bring the pasta mix together to form a rough dough, then transfer to a clean, dry work surface. Knead the dough for about 8 minutes, until smooth and supple. Wrap in cling film (plastic wrap) and put in the fridge for 30 minutes to rest, and ideally for longer as it will get firmer and easier to work with. It will keep for up to 3 days in the fridge, just remove from the fridge 30 minutes before using.

Make the tortellini (see shaping tortellini on page 124).

Make the red wine reduction. Bring the red wine to the boil in a wide-based saucepan, then simmer until it has reduced by three-quarters – you need exactly 50ml (2fl oz/scant ¼ cup), so measure to check and reduce further if needed. Add the mushroom stock and bay leaf and bring to the boil, simmer again until it has reduced by two-thirds in volume – you need exactly 350ml (12fl oz/1½ cups) of reduced stock, so measure to check, and reduce further if necessary.

FOR THE MUSHROOMS

200ml (7fl oz/generous ¾ cup) mushroom stock (see page 63)
4 king oyster mushrooms, base trimmed
250g (9oz) chestnut mushrooms, stalks removed
100g (3½oz) shimeji mushrooms, trimmed and base removed
2 tbsp extra virgin olive oil
sea salt, to sprinkle

FOR THE GARNISH

½ x quantity of cavolo nero crisps (see page 26)

KING OYSTER MUSHROOMS

King oyster mushrooms are large, meaty mushrooms that look a little like porcinis (or ceps) but have a meatier texture and more delicate flavour. They benefit from being a farmable mushroom and so are more readily available than porcinis. If you cannot find any then you can substitute porcinis, pied bleu or even quarters of peeled portobello mushrooms.

When ready to cook, put 4 litres (7 pints/16 cups) of cold water and 40g (1½oz/ 2½ tbsp) of salt in a large lidded saucepan and bring to the boil. Line a baking tray (sheet) with kitchen (paper) towel and have a clean tea towel to keep the cooked tortellini warm.

Cut each king oyster mushroom "log" into 7mm (⅓ inch) slices. Cut each chestnut mushroom in half across the middle to give 2 flat discs, then cut these into 7mm (⅓ inch) discs. Slice the shimeji mushrooms.

Heat 1 tablespoon of olive oil in a small frying pan (skillet) and add the king oyster mushroom slices. Sprinkle with a little salt, brown one side to a golden brown and then flip and colour the other side. Add the mushroom stock and reduce it down to make a glaze, then keep warm.

Heat the remaining olive oil in a frying pan (skillet) and add the chestnut mushrooms, sprinkle with a little salt and fry for 2 minutes. Add the shimeji mushrooms and continue to cook until the liquid has released from the mushrooms and evaporated again. Add 4 tablespoons of the red wine reduction and cook to thicken slightly, then keep warm until needed.

Now cook your pasta. Turn the temperature down so the water is at a gentle simmer. Gently place no more than 5 tortellini into the saucepan of simmering water and stir gently to prevent them from sticking to the base. You need to cook them for only 1–2 minutes – they will float to the surface and the pasta will be firm but cooked – it must have bite. As soon as they are done, carefully remove them, one at a time, using a slotted spoon and put on the lined baking tray (sheet). Cover with a tea towel to keep warm and prepare the next 5. Repeat until they are all cooked. Once they are all cooked place 3–5 tortellini into each of 4 pasta bowls. Spoon the diced mushrooms over the top of each and then arrange the king oyster mushroom slices on top.

Pour the mushroom reduction into the bottom of the bowl. Add a cavolo nero crisp to each bowl and serve immediately.

This is a very simple way to prepare pasta using elements that you may have left over from other recipes: I always have some remnants of fermented cashew, smoked almond butter or pine nut butter and any of them will work in this recipe. Equally, you can use button mushrooms in place of wild mushrooms and – at a push – another stock. You can make your own pasta, as described here, or you can use a good quality shop-bought one.

Serves: 4

TAGLIATELLE
with wild mushrooms

1 batch of hand-rolled pasta dough (see page 125)
semolina, for dusting
400ml (13½fl oz/1⅔ cups) mushroom stock (see page 63)
1 tbsp oil
1kg (2¼lb) wild mushrooms, cleaned and trimmed (not washed)
250ml (8½fl oz/1 cup) dry white wine
4 sprigs of thyme
100g (3½oz) fermented cashews (see page 85) or pine nut butter (see page 221)

I like to roll the pasta dough by hand but if you prefer you can use a pasta machine (see page 124). If you are working by hand then, depending on the size of your worktop and how many you are feeding, you may need to do this in two batches. Roll out the dough using your preferred method until it is the thickness of a credit card or a touch thicker. Leave it on the surface to cure (dry a little) until it is a little leathery and no longer sticky. When one side is cured, flip it over to cure the other side. Dust the dough lightly with semolina and fold over itself two or three times. Using a very sharp knife, cut it into thin strips (about 3-4mm/⅛ inch). Unroll each piece and group them together, sprinkle with a little semolina to prevent sticking and twist into a loose nest shape (if you haven't sufficiently cured your pasta then the strips may stick at this stage; if in doubt try to keep them separate or hang them on a pasta rack or coat hanger instead). Store somewhere to dry while you make your sauce.

To make the mushroom sauce, bring the mushroom stock to the boil in a small pan then simmer gently until it has reduced by half.

Heat a large frying pan (skillet) over a medium-high heat until very hot and add a dash of olive oil. Add the wild mushrooms and fry hard for about 10 minutes until they release their juices and the juices evaporate. Add the wine and thyme and reduce by three-quarters, then add the reduced mushroom stock and fermented cashews (see page 85) or pine nut butter (see page 221) and stir until combined. You are looking for a texture of pancake batter: if it is too thin, simmer for a few minutes, if it is too thick add a splash of pasta cooking water to thin it out.

To serve, bring a large pan of water to the boil and season as for pasta water (see page 125). If reheating the sauce, put it in a medium saucepan and gently heat it on a low heat until just bubbling. Add the pasta to the water at a medium boil until just al dente (if following this recipe, about 30 seconds).

Once the pasta is cooked, remove it from the water with a spider and add it straight into the sauce. Gently stir to combine, then split between 4 pasta bowls and top with a twist of fresh black pepper and a few leaves of fresh thyme.

Italian food is all about simplicity. It is about using fantastic produce, treating it with respect and mastering the tiny details of apparently easy food. Gnocchi is the ultimate expression of this philosophy; it is so simple, yet so hard to do really well.

Almond milk contains starches from the almonds so will thicken naturally when heated. It also thickens further in the presence of an acid. Because of this there is no need to add starch or a roux to your almond sauces, they will thicken nicely all on their own.

Serves: 4

POTATO GNOCCHI
with summer peas and spinach in an almond white wine sauce

FOR THE POTATO GNOCCHI
800g (1lb 12oz) potatoes
(preferably russet or king Edward, baking potatoes as a fall back)
135g (4¾oz/1 cup) type 00 flour (may be more or less if calculating the ratio weight)

FOR THE SAUCE
1 x quantity of almond milk (see page 221)
200g (7oz/1⅓ cups) freshly podded peas
25ml (1fl oz/5 tsp) extra virgin olive oil
1 small onion, finely diced
125ml (4fl oz/½ cup) dry white wine
200ml (7fl oz/generous ¾ cup) basic stock (see page 62)
30ml (1fl oz/2 tbsp) lemon juice
3g (3½ tsp) chopped summer savory or tarragon leaves (optional)
sea salt
100g (3½oz/3⅓ cups) spinach

FOR THE GARNISH
1 lemon
black pepper
white truffle oil

Make the almond milk (see page 221) in advance as the almonds need to soak overnight.

Make the basic stock (see page 62) and the gnocchi (see page 136), weighing out the cooked potato and adding 30 per cent of the cooked weight in flour. Alternatively, use 400g (14oz) of cooked potatoes and 135g (4¾oz/1 cup) of flour.

Blanch the peas for 2–3 minutes then shock in ice-cold water (see page 183) and set aside.

Heat the olive oil in a large saucepan over a low heat. Add the onion and fry gently for about 2 minutes until translucent but not coloured. Add the white wine and simmer gently to reduce by two-thirds, then add the stock and continue to simmer until it has reduced by half. Add the almond milk and simmer gently to thicken. When it is just thick enough to coat the back of a metal spoon, remove from the heat and add the lemon juice and summer savory. Season with salt to taste.

When the sauce is nearly ready, cook the gnocchi (see page 136). Then add the gnocchi, peas and spinach to the sauce and gently warm through. If the sauce has become too thick, dilute with a little water until it is the desired consistency.

Spoon the gnocchi onto 4 plates. Zest a quarter of a lemon over each plate, add a few twists of black pepper and a very generous drizzle of white truffle oil. Serve immediately.

GNOCCHI TROUBLE-SHOOTING

- *If the gnocchi is tough and/or leathery — you kneaded the dough too much.*
- *If the gnocchi is hard — you added too much flour.*
- *If the gnocchi breaks up in the water — you didn't add enough flour.*
- *If the gnocchi cracks as you roll it — you didn't work fast enough and the dough cooled too much. You can knead it to return elasticity, but the end product will be tougher.*
- *If the gnocchi dough is wet and sticky and you've already added lots of flour — you either mashed your potato and made it gluey, chose a wet or buttery variety of potato, or didn't take enough care to get the moisture from the potato.*

| HOW TO MAKE POTATO GNOCCHI |

Most gnocchi recipes you come across outside of Italy contain egg, but within Italy there is a lively debate about whether it should or not. Gnocchi made using just flour and potato is the purest way of working. It creates a beautiful, light gnocchi where the flavour of the potato can really sing through. It also makes it hard to work with. The following will help point you in the right direction, until you develop a feel for it.

- Every potato has a different water content so you can never say for sure how much flour you will need. Add 30 per cent of the cooked potato weight, and then a little more if the mix is still too sticky.

- The variety of potato you buy matters more than anything else: russets and king Edwards are your best choices. Otherwise use baking potatoes as they are selected to be fluffy regardless of their variety.

- Always use a potato ricer to mash the potato. Using a masher will risk making the potato gluey before you've even started, and the potato needs to be light and fluffy.

- Work very fast – the mix is easy to work with while warm and becomes harder and harder as it cools.

- The first time you make gnocchi, it's unlikely to be perfect. Don't worry or give up at the first hurdle, be willing to give it five goes before you become despondent, or try making cavatelli instead (see page 120) to get a feel for it.

- You are not trying to knead the dough as you would knead bread, but merely incorporate the flour as you would for a shortbread. If you knead it, your gnocchi will be tough.

- Buying a ridged pasta board will make your life infinitely easier. You can roll gnocchi on a fork, but it's hard and you'll be there for the rest of your life!

Preheat the oven to (fan) 160°C/180°C/350°F/gas mark 4. Line a small baking tray (sheet) with 200g (7oz/¾ cup) of fine sea salt. Place the potatoes on the salt and cut 3 long slits in the top of each potato. Bake in the oven for 1 hour or until completely soft, then remove and discard the salt.

Holding the potatoes in a tea towel, cut them in half lengthways to allow the steam to escape and leave for 3–4 minutes. Scoop the flesh out and put it through a potato ricer, with the smallest disc inserted. Weigh the potatoes, then work out 30 per cent of that weight, and measure out that amount of flour (for example, for 500g (1lb 2oz) of potato, weigh 150g (5½oz) of flour.

Scatter the potato over a clean work surface and sieve half the flour over the top. With your fingertips, mix the flour in and then sprinkle the remaining flour over the top. Gently fold the mix over to incorporate the flour and press it down to form a smooth, light dough. If it feels very wet or sticky add a little more flour until workable. Knead twice.

Lightly flour your work surface, form the dough into a log and roll it in the flour. Working quickly to prevent the mix from cooling too fast, cut the dough into equal eighths and then roll each piece into a 1cm (½-inch) wide sausage. Cut each sausage into 1.5cm (½-inch) lengths. Keep the rest of the dough under a clean tea towel.

Using the fleshy part of your thumb, flatten each ball slightly against a gnocchi board, butter pat or large fork and then roll it downwards to form a gnocchi shape with a little crease in the bottom where it folded over. Press hard enough to create a ridge, but not so hard you flatten the gnocchi. Allow each gnocchi to roll onto the work surface. If they are a little sticky dust the surface very lightly in fine semolina. When you've made all the gnocchi, spread them out on a board lined with non-stick baking parchment.

Bring a large saucepan with 4 litres (7 pints/16 cups) of water and 40g (1½oz/2½ tbsp) of salt to the boil. When the water is boiling, carefully add the gnocchi in 2 batches. Try not to fiddle with it too much or you risk sticking them together. If you think they may stick to the bottom, stir the water on the surface to form a vortex without touching the gnocchi.

Once the gnocchi float to the surface, cook for a further 30 seconds, then scoop out with a slotted spoon.

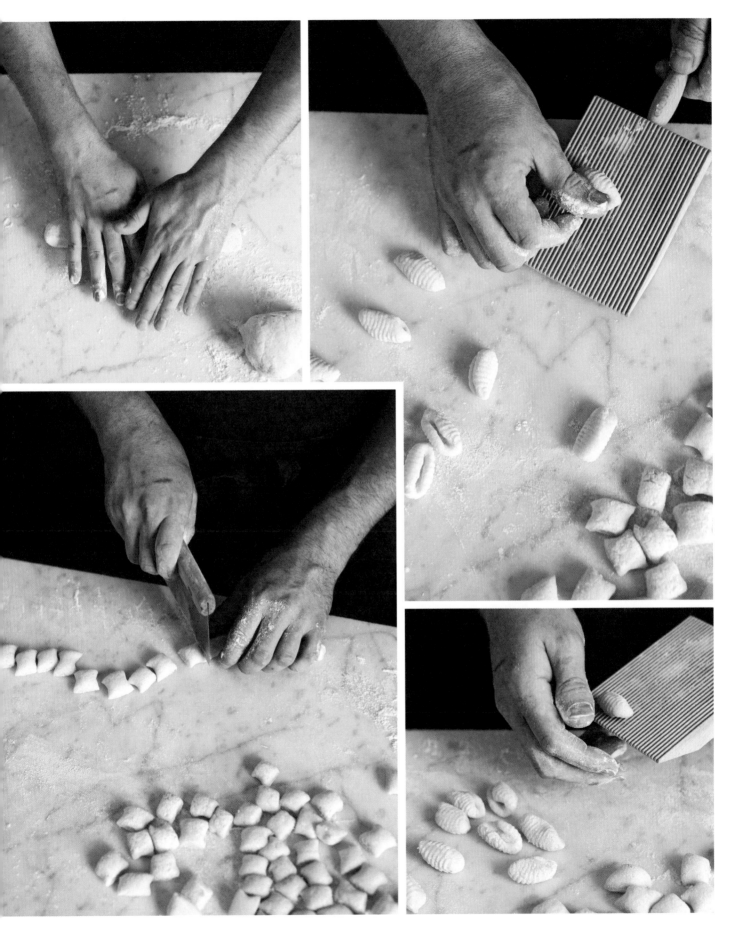

Asparagus lends itself so well to Italian food that sometimes it's hard to think outside of the classic Italian ingredients of lemon, pasta, herbs and garlic. This dish came about from considering asparagus differently, as a fern shoot, just emerging from the earthy bed of the forest floor – woody, nutty and grassy. The gnocchi is a quiet nod to the Italian association it will always hold in my mind.

Serves: 4

HAZELNUT GNOCCHI
with asparagus and a hazelnut sauce

FOR THE GNOCCHI
100g (3½oz/¾ cup) blanched hazelnuts
800g (1lb 12oz) baking potatoes
135g (4¾oz/1 cup) type 00 flour (may be more or less if calculating the ratio weight)
pinch of cayenne pepper

FOR THE SAUCE
50g (1¾oz/⅓ cup) blanched hazelnuts
20ml (4 tsp) extra virgin olive oil
100g (3½oz) sliced shallots
50ml (2fl oz/scant ¼ cup) white wine
15ml (1 tbsp) hazelnut oil
150ml (5fl oz/⅔ cup) cold water
3g (½ tsp) sea salt
cayenne pepper
nutmeg

FOR THE CHERVIL AND ASPARAGUS
1 x quantity of chervil purée (see page 180)
24 asparagus spears, trimmed and peeled

FOR THE GARNISH
15 candied hazelnuts (see page 114), split in half
hazelnut oil, to drizzle

Preheat the oven to (fan) 160°C/180°C/350°F/gas mark 4. Spread the hazelnuts for the gnocchi and the sauce out on 2 separate baking trays (sheets) and roast for 7 minutes until golden. Transfer the nuts for the gnocchi to a blender and process until a flour consistency. Set aside the nuts for the sauce.

Make the chervil purée (see page 180) and candied hazelnuts (see page 114).

Bake and rice the baking potatoes following the method on page 136 for making gnocchi. Weigh the potatoes, then measure out 20 per cent of the weight in the blended hazelnuts and 30 per cent of the weight in flour (see page 136). Alternatively, measure out 400g (14oz) of cooked potatoes, 80g (2¾oz) of blended hazelnuts and 135g (4¾oz) of flour. Make the gnocchi following the method on page 136, then shock in ice-cold water (see page 183), drain and set aside.

Heat the olive oil in a small saucepan and fry the shallots until soft but not coloured. Add the wine and cook until it has evaporated. Put the roasted hazelnuts into a blender with the cooked shallots, hazelnut oil, measured water and salt and process until silky smooth (adding a little water if needed to create a pourable, smooth consistency). Add a tiny pinch of cayenne pepper and a few twists of nutmeg, then pass through a fine sieve into a bowl.

Bring a large saucepan of water to the boil and add a large handful of salt. When boiling, add the asparagus and cook for about 2 minutes until tender, then remove immediately using a slotted spoon and put into a large bowl.

Put the hazelnut gnocchi and hazelnut sauce in a small saucepan and heat gently, adding a little water if necessary to prevent it from becoming too thick and splitting.

Spread 2 tablespoons of chervil purée around the outside of each of 4 large plates. Pile the asparagus in the centre with the gnocchi and sauce next to it. Scatter a few candied hazelnuts over the top, drizzle a little hazelnut oil around the plate and serve.

In the codified world of Italian cookery this wouldn't classify as a risotto, lacking butter and Parmesan cheese, and it certainly wouldn't classify as a risotto Milanese, lacking the addition of bone marrow. However, the idea of a rich, unctuous rice dish flavoured with saffron is a good one and entirely in keeping with food made from plants. Italians would call this a saffron rice, which lacks the romance of the original title, so in recognition of the fact that recipes evolve constantly and if we fix a recipe we kill it, I am going to stick with the original title.

Serves: 4

RISOTTO MILANESE
with peas and pine nuts

2 litres (3½ pints/8 cups) mushroom & fennel stock (see page 63)
50–100g (1¾oz–3½oz) freshly podded peas
3g (½ tsp) sea salt
1g (½ tbsp) saffron
50ml (2fl oz/scant ¼ cup) extra virgin olive oil
2 banana shallots, finely diced
4 cloves of garlic, puréed (see page 145)
400g (14oz/generous 2 cups) carnaroli rice
250ml (8½fl oz/1 cup) white wine
125g (4½oz) pine nut butter (see page 221)
25ml (1fl oz/5 tsp) white truffle oil, plus extra to drizzle
20g (¾oz/2½ tbsp) pine nuts
black pepper

Make the mushroom & fennel stock (see page 63).

Put the peas in a small saucepan, add 200ml (7fl oz/generous ¾ cup) of stock and the salt. Bring to the boil, simmer for 2–4 minutes until the peas are cooked, then remove them with a slotted spoon and leave to cool. When cool, pop the peas out of their skins and set aside. Leave the stock in the saucepan.

Grind the saffron to a powder using a pestle and mortar. Add 50ml (2fl oz/scant ¼ cup) of hot stock, mix well, then set aside.

Heat the olive oil in a saucepan, add the shallot and fry gently until translucent. Add the garlic and fry until cooked, then stir in the rice. Add the wine and cook until completely evaporated. Add 4 ladles of hot stock and cook, stirring constantly, until it has almost disappeared. Add another ladle of stock and continue to stir until it has almost disappeared. Keep adding stock, 1 ladle at a time, until the rice is three-quarters cooked and is thick and stiff – it should be soft but with a chalky texture on the tongue.

Add the saffron stock and keep stirring. Once cooked, remove from the heat and add the pine nut butter and truffle oil. Stir once and allow it to melt into the mix, then vigorously mix it to emulsify the rice. It should be glossy and unctuous, with a just pourable consistency – add a little more stock if needed.

Season the risotto to taste with salt (see page 13) and divide it between the bowls. Scatter over the peas and pine nuts, add a twist of black pepper and a drizzle of white truffle oil, then serve.

This dish heralds the coming of the colder months. The hearty texture of the barley, the bitter radicchio, the hint of smoke from the hazelnuts, a twist of nutmeg, it all comes together into something that is gently seductive, the culinary equivalent of blankets and wine in front of a fire with loved ones.

Serves: 4

PARSNIP BARLEY RISOTTO
with poached pears and smoked hazelnuts

FOR THE POACHED PEARS
2 Williams pears
250ml (8½fl oz/1 cup) basic stock
   (see page 62)
250ml (8½fl oz/1 cup) white wine
2 sprigs of thyme
5g (⅛oz/1 tsp) sea salt
50g (1¾oz/¼ cup) caster
   (superfine) sugar
hazelnut oil, to fry

FOR THE RISOTTO
1 x quantity of parsnip & shallot
   purée (see page 182)
40ml (1½fl oz/8 tsp) extra virgin
   olive oil
40g (1½oz) diced banana shallots
3 cloves of garlic, puréed (see
   opposite page)
200g (7oz/1 cup) pearl barley
225ml (7½fl oz/scant 1 cup) white
   wine
1.5 litres (2½ pints/6 cups) basic
   stock (see page 62)
sea salt

FOR THE ROAST PARSNIPS
2 large parsnips, peeled and
   trimmed
2 sprigs of thyme
1 bay leaf
2 pieces of mace
25ml (1fl oz/5 tsp) extra virgin
   olive oil
good pinch of sea salt

Prepare the basic stock (see page 62), parsnip & shallot purée (see page 182), smoked hazelnuts (see page 114) and pickled pear (see page 98).

Make the poached pears. Peel each pear, cut in half lengthways, then remove the core and stalk. Place the pear halves in a saucepan with the rest of the poaching ingredients (but not the hazelnut oil) and gently bring to the boil. Simmer gently for 5–10 minutes. As soon as the pears are softening – a knife should easily pass through the thickest part – remove from the heat and leave to cool in the saucepan.

Make the barley risotto base. Heat the olive oil in a saucepan, then add the shallot and fry gently until soft. Add the puréed garlic and cook for 2 minutes, then add the pearl barley and stir. Add the wine and cook until it has all evaporated, then add 500ml (18fl oz/2 cups) of stock and bring to the boil. Simmer gently until the stock has almost disappeared, stirring often and vigorously. Add another 250ml (8½fl oz/1 cup) of stock and cook until this has disappeared. Keep adding the stock in batches and cook until the barley is soft but still has a "pop", and the stock has all evaporated. Note you may not need to use all the stock. When ready, transfer to a large baking tray (sheet) and spread out evenly to cool quickly.

Preheat the oven to (fan) 160°C/180°C/350°F/gas mark 4. Put a 45cm (18-inch) strip of baking parchment on a baking tray (sheet). Cut the parsnips into quarters lengthways, then chop to 1cm (½-inch) dice. Mix the parsnip, thyme, bay leaf, mace, olive oil and salt in a large bowl, then transfer the mix to the centre of the paper, fold in half, and roll up the edges to form a sealed parcel. Bake in the oven for 20 minutes until just soft. Remove the parsnip and set aside.

Put the radicchio leaves in a bowl, add a generous glug of hazelnut oil and a pinch of salt and toss well using your fingers.

Halve each smoked hazelnut and place in a small bowl with a little hazelnut oil and a small pinch of salt.

Put the barley risotto into a saucepan and add the parsnip & shallot purée. If very thick, add a little water. Warm gently, stirring. Once hot, check the consistency – it should be pourable but appear thick and creamy. Taste and season with salt (see page 13), then keep warm.

FOR THE RADICCHIO
12 red radicchio leaves
hazelnut oil
sea salt

FOR THE GARNISH
20g (¾oz/2½ tbsp) smoked
  hazelnuts, halved (see page 114),
1 x quantity of pickled pear (see
  page 98)
hazelnut oil
pinch of sea salt
1 nutmeg clove

While you warm the risotto, remove the poached pears from their liquid and pat dry with kitchen (paper) towel. Line a frying pan (skillet) with a sheet of non-stick baking parchment and get it very hot. Add a splash of hazelnut oil and place the pears, cut side down, on the paper. Press down and cook at a high temperature until the surface is very dark, almost burnt. Remove from the pan and cut a slice from the back of each pear so it will sit up at an angle. Place just off centre on each of 4 large plates.

Check the risotto consistency, adding a little more water if too thick. Fold half the diced parsnip mix into the risotto. Spoon 1 tablespoon of risotto mix next to each pear. Lay a radicchio leaf on top, then add another 4 tablespoons of risotto on top of the leaf. Add another radicchio leaf and another 4 tablespoons of risotto then top with a radicchio leaf. Scatter the hazelnuts over the plate, then scatter the remaining diced parsnip over the top. Place 7 pieces of pickled pear across each plate and drizzle over hazelnut oil. Finely grate a little nutmeg over the top and serve.

PURÉEING GARLIC

I don't recommend using garlic crushers/presses, so this is my tried and tested way of puréeing garlic. Using a large knife, cut the woody root end from the clove. Place the flat side of the knife's blade against the garlic and crush the clove until you hear a crunch. The clove should now come cleanly away from the skin. Discard the skin and on a chopping board slice the garlic as thinly as you can, then chop it as finely as you can. Bring it into a small pile and sprinkle with a large pinch of salt. With the flat of the blade, crush the pile of garlic and draw it towards you, smearing it against the board. Collect it all back up into a pile and crush and smear it again. Continue doing this until you have a smooth purée.

A good mushroom risotto should have a lot of mushrooms and a lot of umami (see page 14) – this version has both.

The trick to really well-cooked mushrooms is to use a large pan and a high heat so they don't stew in their own juices. Try to cook the mushrooms alongside the risotto mix so you can combine them when the rice is ready.

Serves: 4

PERFECT MUSHROOM RISOTTO

FOR THE DOUBLE MUSHROOM STOCK
1.5 litres (2½ pints/6¼ cups) mushroom stock (see page 63)
50g (1¾oz) dried shiitake or porcini mushrooms

FOR THE MUSHROOM PURÉE
40ml (1½fl oz/8 tsp) extra virgin olive oil
190g (6¾oz) chestnut mushrooms, sliced
115ml (4fl oz/½ cup) ruby port
30g (1¼oz) dried mushrooms (reserved from the double mushroom stock)
12ml (2½ tsp) red wine vinegar
15ml (1 tbsp) truffle oil
45ml (1½fl oz/3 tbsp) double mushroom stock (reserved from above)

FOR THE RISOTTO
2 king oyster mushrooms
200g (7oz) chestnut mushrooms
2 large portobello mushrooms
1 head shimeji mushrooms
75ml (2¾fl oz/⅓ cup) extra virgin olive oil
sea salt
100g (3½oz/½ cup) diced banana shallots
4 cloves of garlic, puréed (see page 145)
350g (12oz/1¾ cups) carnaroli rice
double mushroom stock (see above)

First make the mushroom stock (see page 63), then the double mushroom stock. In a saucepan bring the mushroom stock to the boil, then remove from the heat. Add the dried mushrooms, cover with a lid and leave for 30 minutes. Drain the stock into a separate saucepan and set aside. Reserve the dried mushrooms for the mushroom purée.

Make the mushroom purée. Heat the olive oil in a wide-based saucepan. Add the chestnut mushrooms and sweat until the juices have evaporated. Add the ruby port and reduce until a thick syrup. Remove from the heat and transfer to a blender. Add the rest of the ingredients to the blender and blend until silky smooth, adding a little water only if necessary.

Prepare and cook the mushrooms for the risotto. Cut the king oyster mushrooms into 5mm (¼-inch) slices. Quarter the chestnut mushrooms, slice the portobello mushrooms and trim the woody base from the shimeji mushrooms. To cook the fried mushrooms, heat 50ml (2fl oz/scant ¼ cup) of olive oil in a large, deep frying pan (skillet). Add the oyster mushrooms and cook for 2 minutes. Add the chestnut mushrooms and a small pinch of salt and cook for 1 minute. Add the portobello mushrooms with another small pinch of salt and cook for about 4 minutes until all the mushrooms are three-quarters cooked. Add the shimeji mushrooms and cook until all the mushrooms are cooked through (but not withered) and all the liquid is gone. Adjust the seasoning (see page 13).

Once the mushrooms are on the go, cook the rest of the risotto. Heat the double mushroom stock in a saucepan and bring to a gentle simmer. Heat the remaining olive oil in a frying pan (skillet), add the shallot and fry gently until translucent. Add the garlic and fry until cooked, then add the rice and stir well. Add 4 ladles of hot stock and cook, stirring constantly, until it has almost disappeared. Add another ladle of stock and continue to stir until it has almost disappeared. Keep adding stock, 1 ladle at a time, until the rice is nearly but not quite cooked through, about 15–20 minutes. You may not need all the stock, or you may need to add a little extra hot water. The texture will be thick, creamy and stiff.

When the risotto is cooked, add the fried mushrooms and remove from the heat. Add the mushroom purée and stir well to combine. Taste and adjust the seasoning (see page 13), divide between 4 bowls and serve.

Broccoli has a majestic shape and a deep, satisfying flavour when cooked well. The standard way of preparing broccoli by cutting off the florets and discarding the stem is such a waste as the stem is just as edible as the flower heads. Preparing it this way, which has become my go-to technique, not only shows off its dramatic shape but also delivers a broad surface area for the Maillard reaction to take place (see page 175), resulting in a striking, delicious plate of food. Just remember to allow time to soak the spelt and lettuce.

Serves: 4

SEARED CALABRESE BROCCOLI
with spelt grain, a smoked almond emulsion and candied almonds

FOR THE SPELT GRAIN
300g (10½oz/1¾ cups) pearled
   spelt grain
500ml (18fl oz/2 cups) water
5g (⅛oz/1 tsp) sea salt

FOR THE COS LETTUCE
1.25g (¼ tsp) sea salt
250ml (8½fl oz/1 cup) cold water
1 cos lettuce head

FOR THE BROCCOLI
1 large broccoli head
oil, for frying
sea salt

FOR THE SMOKED ALMOND EMULSION
25g (1oz/2¾ tbsp) smoked almonds
   (see page 114)
25g (1oz/3 tbsp) smoked cashew
   nuts (see page 114)
90ml (3¼fl oz/generous ⅓ cup)
   high-quality olive oil
100ml (3½fl oz/scant ½ cup) water
1.5g (¼ tsp) sea salt
pinch of cayenne pepper

FOR THE GARNISH
4 tbsp drained pickled cabbage
   (see page 98) or sauerkraut
   (see page 99)
candied almonds (see page 114)
12 lovage leaves, coarsely shredded

Put the spelt into a bowl, cover with cold water and leave to soak for at least 4 hours – and ideally overnight – in the fridge.

Mix the salt and water together for the cos lettuce and leave so the salt dissolves completely into the water to make a saline solution. Remove and discard the outer 3 or 4 leaves from the lettuce. Cut the lettuce into quarters lengthways and submerge in the saline solution. Place in the fridge for at least 4 hours – or ideally overnight.

Prepare the pickled cabbage (see page 98), candied almonds (see page 114), smoked almonds (see page 114) and smoked cashew nuts (see page 114).

Drain and rinse the spelt, then put into a small saucepan with the measured water and salt. Cover with a lid, bring to the boil, then simmer gently for about 10 minutes until the spelt is soft but still pops in the mouth. Drain and rinse in cold water.

Meanwhile, peel the stalk of the broccoli, removing any woody parts. Cut the broccoli in half through the centre of the stalk. Cut each half in half again through the centre of the stalk and then again to give 8 wedges. Using a peeler, neaten up each wedge.

Put all the smoked almond emulsion ingredients together in a blender and process until silky smooth and glossy.

Take the cos lettuce out of the saline solution. Select 8 lettuce leaves and cut them in half, forming sharp wedges. Form the pickled cabbage into 4 neat balls.

Heat a little oil in a large frying pan (skillet). Fry the broccoli wedges on each side, seasoning well with salt, until dark and crispy. Cover with a lid and remove from the heat. Set aside for 4 minutes to soften in their own steam.

Put the spelt and smoked almond emulsion into a small saucepan and heat gently until hot, but do not boil. Check and adjust the seasoning and keep warm.

Put 6 tablespoons of spelt mix in each of 4 large pasta bowls. Place 1 or 2 wedges of cooked broccoli upright on top of the spelt and add a ball of pickled cabbage. Add 2 shards of lettuce and then scatter with candied almonds and shredded lovage leaves. Serve hot.

Before I made the decision to go completely plant-based this was one of my favourite snacks, reminiscent of lazy mornings in Spain drinking strong bitter coffee and looking out across the mountains. I decided to create my own version of tortilla after being served so many sad, limp imitations in vegan cafés along with that other poorly made vegan classic, the farinita. This dish is a hybrid: it takes the technique from a tortilla de patatas and the flavour and depth from a well-made farinita. Dare I say it, I think I prefer this to the classic, egg-bound version, and it certainly keeps better for the next day. Just make sure you prepare the gram flour batter a day or two ahead.

Serves: 4–8

TORTILLA DE PATATAS
with crushed tomato salad

FOR THE TORTILLA
100g (3½oz/scant 1 cup) gram flour
150ml (5fl oz/⅔ cup) water
800g (1lb 12oz) floury potatoes (baking, maris piper or rooster work well)
500–750ml (18–26ml/2–3 cups) olive oil
1 brown onion, sliced
5g (⅛oz/1 tsp) sea salt

FOR THE SALAD
4 large, ripe, sweet tomatoes (the best you can buy)
15ml (1 tbsp) olive oil
5ml (1 tsp) sherry vinegar
1g (scant ¼ tsp) sea salt
1 small shallot (not a banana shallot), finely diced
10 tarragon leaves, diced

TO SERVE
everyday bread (see page 214)

Sieve the gram flour into a small sterile jug (see page 99) and whisk in the water to form a smooth batter. Put somewhere warm (22°C/71°F) for 24–48 hours. The longer the fermentation time, the better the flavour.

When ready to cook, prepare the tomato salad. Blanch, shock and peel the tomatoes (see page 82), then cut into 5mm (¼-inch) dice. Put in a small bowl with the oil, sherry vinegar and salt. Crush gently with a fork, then add the shallot and tarragon. Stir everything together and set aside for the flavours to mingle.

Cut the unpeeled potatoes into 1cm (½-inch) dice and place in a saucepan. Completely cover with the olive oil. Gently heat the oil until it starts to boil, stirring gently to prevent the potatoes from sticking. Once the oil is bubbling, add the onion and simmer, gently stirring often, for 10–15 minutes until the potato is cooked. Once cooked, immediately pour the mix through a sieve set over a saucepan, allowing all the oil to drip through. While the potato is piping hot, tip into a large bowl, stir in the salt and add the gram flour batter. Stir to mix well.

Put a couple of tablespoons of the oil into a non-stick 23cm (9-inch) frying pan (skillet) and heat gently. When hot, tip the potato mix into the pan, flatten it down and press to make sure there are no gaps. Fry gently until firm and the bottom is golden brown.

Make sure the tortilla is loose in the pan, then firmly holding a plate over the top, turn the pan over to deposit the tortilla on the plate. Slide the tortilla back into the frying pan (skillet) and fry until the underside is golden brown. Turn out onto a board and allow to cool to room temperature before cutting into slices and serving with the crushed tomato salad and bread.

This dish is the epitome of autumn: rich, creamy and indulgent, with deep earthy flavours and a hint of woodland about it. It is perfect for when the leaves are beginning to drop and you light the fire for the first time.

Serves: 4

BEETROOT AND MUSHROOM CASSEROLE
with hazelnut polenta

8 beetroots (beets), peeled (taking care to preserve the shape of each beetroot)

50ml (2fl oz/scant ¼ cup) rapeseed oil

2 onions, sliced

4 cloves of garlic, pureed

400g (14oz) chestnut mushrooms, cleaned and halved

375ml (12½fl oz/generous 1½ cups) red wine

375ml (12½fl oz/generous 1½ cups) mushroom stock (see page 63)

2 bay leaves

4 sprigs of thyme

2 sprigs of rosemary

100g (3½oz) cavolo nero or chard

40g (1½oz) roasted hazelnuts, to serve

FOR THE HAZELNUT POLENTA

750ml (26fl oz/3 cups) mushroom stock (see page 63)

150g (5½oz/scant 1 cup) polenta (cornmeal)

200g (7oz) hazelnut butter (see page 221)

8g (¼oz/1½ tsp) sea salt

Preheat the oven to (fan) 160°C/180°C/350°F/gas mark 4.

Carefully cut each beetroot (beet) into halves and quarters – you want each piece to look like 2 mouthfuls.

Heat the rapeseed oil in an ovenproof casserole dish (pan) over a medium heat, add the sliced onion and sweat gently until the slices are jelly-like and slightly coloured. Add the garlic and cook for a few minutes, then add the mushrooms and cook until they release their juices and the juices have evaporated. Add the wine and beetroots (beets) and simmer until the wine has reduced by half, then add the mushroom stock and herbs, cover with the casserole lid and bake in the oven for 45 minutes.

Remove from the oven and check the beetroots (beets): a knife should pass through them like butter. If there is still a lot of liquid, put the pot on the hob and simmer gently until the broth thickens and looks rich and inviting. If the mix looks dry, add a splash of water at a time until a thick sauce forms. Add the shredded cavolo nero or chard and heat gently until it is wilted and cooked. Keep warm while you prepare your hazelnut polenta.

To make the polenta, heat the mushroom stock in a saucepan until simmering gently. Slowly sprinkle the polenta (cornmeal) into the stock, whisking all the time. As soon as the mix thickens (it will take a matter of seconds), remove from the heat and stir in the hazelnut butter and salt. Whisk to make sure the butter is fully incorporated and looks thick and glossy. Taste and adjust the seasoning if needed (see page 13).

Lay out 4 large rimmed plates or pasta bowls. Divide the polenta among the plates evenly and create a well in the centre using a spoon, to hold the casserole. Spoon the beetroots (beets) and mushrooms on top of the polenta and scatter the roasted hazelnuts over the top. Serve while piping hot.

A daag is a simple home curry base that you can make in large quantities and store in batches in the freezer, ready to make a quick, simple meal whenever you want. Use this recipe a jumping-off point and make it your own: I add smoked almond butter to create a richer and more luxurious flavour and texture, and the cauliflower fritters (see page 25) offer a more complex version, but there is nothing stopping you from adding raw cauliflower florets and cooking them in the sauce. I use chickpeas (garbanzo beans) because, when you are using a lot of aquafaba, you need to find as many uses for chickpeas as possible but you could substitute them for any beans (I love mung beans in this). Substitute the masala mix for a good quality garam masala if you prefer.

The masala mix is best made fresh, though it keeps for months (the longer you keep it the more it will lose its lighter brighter flavours and the more woody, musty flavours will come to the fore).

Serves: 4

CAULIFLOWER DAAG
with cauliflower rice

FOR THE MASALA MIX
6g (⅛oz/2 tsp) cumin seeds
4g (2 tsp) coriander seeds
8g (¼oz/1½ tsp) fenugreek seeds
4g (2 tsp) fennel seeds
12 green cardamom pods
8 black cardamom pods
4g (2 tsp) black peppercorns
1g (scant ¼ tsp) asafoetida
2 cloves
2 star anise
½ nutmeg
7.5cm (3-inch) piece of cinnamon
   stick

FOR THE DAAG CURRY BASE
2cm (¾-inch) piece of organic
   ginger (see page 58)
3 cloves of garlic
1 red chilli
3 tomatoes
70ml (2½fl oz/generous ¼ cup)
   rapeseed oil
2 onions, sliced
10g salt
3.5g (1½ tsp) freshly ground
   coriander
0.5g (⅛ tsp) freshly ground cumin

Preheat the oven to (fan) 160°C/180°C/350°F/gas mark 4.

To make the masala mix, put the cumin, coriander, fenugreek and fennel seeds on a small baking tray (sheet) and roast for 5 minutes until fragrant and a shade darker. Remove the cardamom seeds from their black and green pods and discard the pods. Put all the spices in a spice grinder, or (if you have strong wrists) a pestle and mortar, and grind to a fine powder. Store in an airtight jar until needed.

To make the curry base, mince the ginger, garlic and chilli together by hand or using a blender. Purée the tomatoes in a blender (separately, after removing the ginger, garlic and chilli from the blender).

Heat the oil in a medium saucepan over a low-medium heat. Add the onions and salt and fry for until caramelised and dark brown – this could take up to 20 minutes. Add the ginger, chilli and garlic purée and cook for a few minutes, then add the ground coriander and cook for 5 minutes. Add the remaining spices and cook for 30 seconds, then add the tomato and fresh coriander (cilantro) and water and cook for 20 minutes. Stir in the smoked almond butter and blend to a smooth sauce.

0.5g (⅛ tsp) ground turmeric

1g (scant ¼ tsp) spice mix (such as garam masala)

15g (½oz) fresh coriander (cilantro) leaves, chopped

250g (8½fl oz/1 cup) water

50g (1¾oz) smoked almond butter (see below)

FOR THE CORIANDER RICE

400g (14oz) basmati rice

20ml (4 tsp) rapeseed oil

5g (⅛oz/2½ tsp) cumin seeds

8g (¼oz/1½ tsp) sea salt

510ml (17fl oz/generous 2 cups) water

TO SERVE

200g (7oz) cooked chickpeas (garbanzo beans)

8 fresh tomatoes, chopped

500g (1lb 2oz) spinach

Cauliflower fritters (see page 25)

FOR THE SMOKED ALMOND BUTTER

50g (1¾oz) blanched almonds

50g (1¾oz) cashew pieces

60ml (2¼fl oz/¼ cup) extra virgin olive oil

80ml (3fl oz/⅓ cup) cold water

2g (⅓ tsp) salt

pinch of cayenne pepper

To make the coriander (cilantro) rice, put the basmati rice in a bowl and cover with cold water. Gently agitate the rice with your fingers to wash it and carefully pour off the cloudy water. Cover it in cold water again and repeat the process 4 or 5 more times until the water remains clear. Cover with cold water one more time and leave to soak for 2 hours. Strain and rinse under the cold tap.

Put the oil and cumin seeds in a saucepan and heat gently until the cumin is a shade darker. Add the rice and salt and stir through, then add the water and cover. Simmer gently for 20 minutes until you start to hear the rice clicking in the pan. Check the rice and if all the water has been absorbed then leave it for 5 minutes to steam with the lid on.

When you are ready to serve, stir the chickpeas, additional tomatoes and spinach through the curry base and heat gently. Serve with cauliflower fritters (see page 25) and the coriander (cilantro) rice.

SMOKED ALMOND BUTTER

This is a fantastically useful thing to have in the fridge. You can add it to any sauce to give a complex depth of flavour along with a rich creaminess. Try substituting it in any of the pasta recipes for the pine nut butter (see page 221) or fermented cashew (see page 85). It will keep for up to 3 days in the fridge, or in the freezer for up to 3 months.

Line a stove-top smoker with foil and put the nuts inside, spreading them out evenly. Follow the manufacturer's instructions and smoke gently on a medium heat until deep golden brown, taking care not to burn them. Blend in a high-speed blender with the rest of the ingredients until very, very smooth and pass through a sieve.

This nut roast is very special – it really tastes of nuts, and the gravy is made using long, slow cooking methods to achieve a beautiful depth and complexity of flavour. It is a lot of work to make all the elements, but they can each be made up to three days ahead and reheated when needed. Or you can make just the nut roast and gravy and add accompaniments of your choice.

Serves: 4

HAZELNUT ROAST

with cider apples, braised celeriac (celery root), potato galette and cider gravy

FOR THE NUT ROAST

1 large celeriac (celery root)
    (at least 900g/2lb to give
    500g (1lb 2oz) peeled)
1 large onion
2 cloves of garlic, peeled but whole
25ml (1fl oz/5 tsp) rapeseed oil
8g (¼oz/1½ tsp) sea salt
100g (3½oz/¾ cup) hazelnuts
100g (3½oz/¾ cup) cashew nuts
50g (1¾oz/⅓ cup) sunflower seeds
30g (1¼oz/¼ cup) cornflour
    (cornstarch)
15g (½oz/1 tbsp) caraway mustard
    (see page 39), or shop-bought
    wholegrain mustard
⅛ nutmeg, grated
rapeseed oil

FOR THE POTATO GALETTE

4 baking potatoes
1 onion, peeled
8g (¼oz/1½ tsp) sea salt
150ml (5fl oz/⅔ cup) water
rapeseed oil

FOR THE CIDER GRAVY

25ml (1fl oz/5 tsp) rapeseed oil
1 onion, sliced
1 leek, sliced
250g (9oz) button mushrooms,
    sliced
1 turnip, peeled and sliced
4 cloves of garlic, skin on, smashed
0.5g (¼ tsp) caraway seeds
15g (½oz/1¼ tbsp) caster
    (superfine) sugar
15ml (1 tbsp) cider vinegar

Preheat the oven to (fan) 160°C/180°C/350°F/gas mark 4. Prepare the garlic parsley oil (see page 220).

Prepare the nut roast. Peel the celeriac (celery root) and onion and cut into 2cm (¾-inch) chunks. Place in a large bowl along with the garlic, rapeseed oil and 3g (½ tsp) of the salt. Mix everything together, then spread out on a large baking tray (sheet). Cover the tray with tin foil and roast the celeriac (celery root) in the oven for 30–40 minutes until soft.

Meanwhile, put the hazelnuts and cashews on a baking tray (sheet) and roast for 7 minutes or until golden. Put the sunflower seeds in a frying pan (skillet) with a splash of oil and fry until dark golden. Transfer the seeds to a food processor, process until fine crumbs, then put in a large bowl. Put the cashews and hazelnuts in the food processor and pulse to a coarse crumb, with some lumps, then add to the sunflower seeds. Put the onions, garlic and celeriac into the food processor and pulse to a coarse mash. Add to the nuts and seeds and mix everything together. Add the cornflour (cornstarch), mustard, remaining 5g (1 tsp) of salt and grated nutmeg and mix well.

Lay out a 45cm (18-inch) strip of cling film (plastic wrap), then lay another strip on top. Spoon a quarter of the mix onto this and form into a rough sausage shape about 4cm (1½ inches) thick. Fold over the bottom edge of the cling film (plastic wrap) and roll the mix up to form a sausage about 3cm (1¼ inches) thick. Fold the cling film (plastic wrap) over and roll the sausage tightly in the cling film (plastic wrap). Twist one end of the cling film (plastic wrap) to tie it closed. Squeeze the air out of the other side and twist the other end to form a tight, round, water-tight sausage shape with no air pockets. Tie closed. Repeat with the remaining mix to make 4 sausages in total.

Bring a large saucepan of water to the boil and add the sausages. Turn down to a simmer and cook for 20 minutes, then remove one at a time and plunge into a bowl of ice-cold water. Once cool, transfer to the fridge for at least an hour but ideally overnight, to firm up.

Make the galette. Slice the potatoes and onion very finely on a mandolin, then transfer to a bowl with the salt. Mix well and leave for 30 minutes until soft and pliable.

Line a 900g (2lb) rectangular loaf tin (pan) with baking parchment and layer the potatoes right up to the top. Season well. Add the measured water and cover tightly with foil. Bake for 45 minutes or until a knife passes cleanly through the centre.

250ml (8½fl oz/1 cup) cider
20g (¾oz/4 tsp) tomato purée
2.5g (½ tsp) yeast extract (such as marmite), or 5ml (1 tsp) soy sauce)
750ml (26fl oz/3 cups) water, plus extra for flour paste
1 bay leaf
20g (¾oz) dried mushrooms
3g (½ tsp) sea salt
cornflour (cornstarch)

FOR THE CELERIAC (CELERY ROOT)

1 large celeriac (celery root) (at least 1kg/2¼lb) or several smaller ones, skin and roots removed
100ml (3½fl oz/scant ½ cup) cider gravy (see above)
100ml (3½fl oz/scant ½ cup) water
3g (½ tsp) sea salt

FOR THE CIDER-POACHED APPLES

150g (5½oz/¾ cup) caster (superfine) sugar
150ml (5fl oz/⅔ cup) water
250ml (8½fl oz/1 cup) dry cider
3g (½ tsp) sea salt
3 Granny Smith apples (or other tart variety), peeled

FOR THE BRUSSELS SPROUTS

1 tbsp rapeseed oil
20 Brussels sprouts, trimmed, cut in half and outer leaves discarded
sea salt
2 tbsp garlic parsley oil (see page 220)

Remove from the oven and carefully press down on the foil to compress it. Set aside to cool, then place in the fridge for 2 hours.

Make the cider gravy. Heat the rapeseed oil in a large saucepan until very hot, then add all the sliced vegetables, the garlic and the caraway seeds. Stir well and fry, stirring occasionally, on a high heat for up to 20 minutes until it begins to take a dark colour. While this is cooking, put the sugar in a heavy-bottomed saucepan and heat gently until it melts and forms a golden caramel. Add the vinegar and cook until it evaporates by half, then add the cider and stir.

Add the tomato purée and yeast extract to the saucepan with the vegetables. Stir well and then cook for 5–10 minutes until a crust begins to form on the bottom of the saucepan (do not let this burn). Deglaze the saucepan by adding the sugar and cider mix and stir until the crust has dissolved, then bring to the boil and simmer until the cider has reduced by half. Add the water, bay leaf, dried mushrooms and salt and simmer for 30 minutes. Remove from the heat and leave to infuse for 30 minutes.

Make the cider-poached apples. Put the sugar, water, cider and salt into a small saucepan and bring to the boil. Using a parisienne cutter (melon baller) scoop as many balls of apple as you can from each apple, taking care not to get the woody core. Turn the cider mix down to a gentle simmer and add the apple balls. Simmer very gently until just beginning to soften, then remove from the heat and leave to cool.

Once the cider gravy has infused, strain into another saucepan, measure, and bring to the boil. Boil to reduce the sauce to a quarter of its measured volume. Measure the reduction. For every 250ml (8½fl oz/1 cup) of reduction, mix 10g (¼oz/1¼ tbsp) of cornstarch (corn flour) with 20ml (4 tsp) of cold water. Mix the flour paste in and heat gently, stirring to prevent it sticking, until it has thickened. Taste the sauce and adjust the seasoning with salt if needed (see page 13). Keep warm until needed.

Prepare the braised celeriac (celery root). Preheat the oven to (fan) 160°C/180°C/350°F/gas mark 4. Cut the celeriac into 1cm (½-inch) slices, then cut these into neat triangles or squares. Put them into a small casserole pot and pour the measured cider gravy, water and salt over the top. Bake in the oven for 40 minutes until they are almost melting.

At the same time, slice the galette into 1cm (½-inch) slices. Line a baking tray (sheet) with baking parchment and drizzle it with rapeseed oil. Place the slices of potato galette on it so they are covered with oil on the bottom side. Brush the top side generously with rapeseed oil and bake in the oven for 20 minutes. After 20 minutes turn over each slice – you want an even crispy golden brown colouring all over – and bake for another 10 minutes.

Remove the cling film (plastic wrap) from the nut roast, trim off the ends and cut into 1.5cm (½-inch) thick slices. Line a baking tray (sheet) with baking parchment and lay the nut roast slices on it. Drizzle oil over each slice and put into the oven for 25 minutes to warm through and crisp up.

Heat the rapeseed oil for the Brussels sprouts in a wide saucepan and add the sprouts, cut side down, with a generous pinch of salt. Fry until they go a dark golden colour and then add the garlic parsley oil. Toss to evenly cover them and then turn down the heat and gently cook for 2–4 minutes. Remove from the heat and cover the saucepan with a lid or plate so they steam in their own juices for 4 minutes.

Lay 3 slices of nut roast on each of 4 large dinner plates to form a stacked line. Add a piece of potato galette, 2 pieces of braised celeriac, 3 or 4 apple pieces and the Brussels sprouts on each plate. Generously drizzle cider gravy over everything and serve hot.

Fennel and tomatoes, it's the taste of sunshine, of hot summer days and lazy afternoons. The chickpeas (garbanzo beans) take us to the Mediterranean and northern Africa, and the pistachios over the Suez and into the Middle East.

Serves: 4

LEMON BRAISED FENNEL
with Spanish chickpeas (garbanzo beans) in a smoked tomato sauce

FOR THE BRAISED FENNEL

4 fennel bulbs
100ml (3½fl oz/scant ½ cup) extra
    virgin olive oil
2 ripe plum tomatoes
4 lemon zest strips
10ml (2 tsp) lemon juice
150ml (5fl oz/⅔ cup) water
2 star anise
8g (¼oz/1½ tsp) sea salt

FOR THE FENNEL CREAM

200g (7oz) fennel offcuts (from the
    braised fennel, above)
50ml (2fl oz/scant ¼ cup) extra
    virgin olive oil
1 star anise
sea salt
cayenne pepper

**FOR THE CHICKPEAS
(GARBANZO BEANS)**

400g (14oz) plum tomatoes
50ml (2fl oz/scant ¼ cup) extra
    virgin olive oil, plus extra for
    tomatoes
2 banana shallots, sliced
25ml (1fl oz/5 tsp) high-quality
    extra virgin olive oil
sea salt
cayenne pepper
400g (14oz/2⅔ cups) top-quality
    cooked Spanish chickpeas
    (garbanzo beans) (or canned)

TO SERVE

pistachio pâté (see page 64)
pistachio dukkah (see page 113)
carta di musica (see page 210)

First make the pistachio pâté (see page 64), pistachio dukkah (see page 113) and carta di musica (see page 210).

Preheat the oven to (fan) 140°C/160°C/310°F/gas mark 2½. Trim the fennel stalk and fronds, then cut the fennel lengthways across the middle through the centre of the stem to make "steaks" of fennel held together by the stem. Cut each half into 2 x 1cm (½-inch) slices, so you have 8 thick slices. Reserve the offcuts for the fennel cream.

Heat 60ml (2¼fl oz/¼ cup) of the olive oil in a casserole dish on the hob and add the fennel. Stew gently until the fennel starts to brown. Add the whole tomatoes, lemon zest and juice, measured water, star anise and salt and put the lid on. Put into the oven and leave to stew for 45–60 minutes until the fennel is tender. Remove from the oven and discard the lemon zest and star anise. Drizzle the remaining olive oil over the top, then leave to cool.

Make the fennel cream. Cut the fennel into rough 1cm (½-inch) dice. Gently heat the olive oil in a small saucepan and add the star anise, fennel and a pinch of salt. Turn down the heat and cover with a cartouche (see page 182). Cook very slowly for 30 minutes until very soft. Transfer the contents to a blender and purée until a beautiful creamy consistency. Test for seasoning and add a little cayenne pepper (see page 13).

Make the smoked tomato sauce for the chickpeas (garbanzo beans). Cut the tomatoes in half and toss in a little olive oil. Put 1 tbsp of hickory chips into a stove-top smoker. Place the tomatoes on the smoking grate cut side up. Following the manufacturer's instructions, smoke the tomatoes until cooked with a smoky flavour (see also page 114). Sauté the shallots gently in the regular olive oil until soft but not coloured. Put the shallots and tomatoes into a blender and blend until very smooth. Add the high-quality olive oil and blend briefly to emulsify. Pass through a sieve and season with salt and cayenne pepper (see page 13).

Heat the chickpeas (garbanzo beans) and smoked tomato sauce together in a saucepan gently until hot and thick. At the same, time remove the fennel from its cooking liquid and put into a large frying pan (skillet). Heat gently until it starts to colour, then add about 4 tbsp of the cooking liquid and boil until the liquid has evaporated. Keep warm. Remove the tomatoes from the fennel liquid, cut in half and remove the skins.

Put 2 tablespoons of fennel cream together on each of 4 large plates, spread them out slightly then spread across the plate. Add 2 overlapping slices of pistachio pâté, a piece of fennel and a pile of the tomato and chickpea (garbanzo bean) mix. Then add another piece of fennel and a tomato on top of the chickpea (garbanzo bean) mix. Sprinkle pistachio dukkah over the top and serve hot with carta di musica.

This dish is a great way of making use of a couple of leftovers: the pangrattato is fried breadcrumbs from a stale loaf – a fantastic thing to have on hand to sprinkle on almost everything that needs a bit of texture – and the maltagliati is essentially pasta offcuts. When you are making a lot of pasta you get left with lots of bits that weren't quite the right fit; let them dry out and keep them in a pile and you have a quick, easy, free lunch. Obviously, if you aren't making a lot of pasta then you can just roll out a batch of your favourite pasta and cut it into raggedy shape or alternatively just use your favourite store-bought dried pasta or break up some dried lasagne sheets.

Serves: 4

AUBERGINE (EGGPLANT) RAGU
with pangrattato and maltagliati

FOR THE PANGRATTATO
250g (9oz) stale bread
4 cloves of garlic
extra virgin olive oil

FOR THE SEMOLINA PASTA
400g (14oz/2⅓ cups) fine semolina
235g (8⅓oz) warm water

FOR THE RAGU
75ml (2¾fl oz/⅓ cup) extra virgin olive oil, plus a little extra if needed
2 aubergines (eggplants), cut into 1cm (½-inch) dice
500g (2¼lb) plum tomatos
1 medium onion, diced
2 cloves of garlic
½ red chilli
2g marjoram leaves
sea salt and freshly ground black pepper

To make the pangrattato, blitz your stale bread in a food processor or blender to make breadcrumbs – the bigger the crumb the more crunch you get, just remember there is a line somewhere between breadcrumb and crouton. Purée the garlic, add it to the breadcrumbs and rub it in until all the crumbs are coated. Heat a couple of tablespoons of oil in a frying pan (skillet), add the breadcrumbs and fry gently until golden and crispy. Turn onto a baking tray (sheet) to cool and store in an airtight container until needed.

To make the pasta, put the semolina in a pile on a clean work surface. Make a well in the middle and carefully pour in the water, being sure not to let any spill out. Using a fork, whisk the water around, allowing the semolina to fall into the middle slowly. When it reaches the thickness of pancake batter, swap the fork for a dough scraper and chop in the remaining semolina to form a rough dough. Using your hand, bring it together into a rough ball and knead it a couple of times until homogenous but still dimpled and not smooth. Cover with a bowl and leave for 30 minutes to rest.

Knead again; it should become very smooth and silky very quickly. Form it back into a ball, wrap in cling film (plastic wrap), and leave to rest at room temperature for at least 2 hours before using. You can keep it in the fridge overnight, but it will become sticky and harder to work.

When ready to use, either roll the dough by hand using a rolling pin on a lightly floured surface, until it is just a little thinner than a credit card, or roll through a pasta machine following the instructions on page 124. Cut it into rough pieces and leave scattered on the work surface to dry until you need them.

To make the ragu, heat the olive oil in a large saucepan over a medium heat, add the aubergine (eggplant) and cook for up to around 45 minutes until it is broken down to a mush, catching on the pan, browning and existing in the space between dice and purée: be patient, it's the key to the flavour of this sauce. Remove the aubergine (eggplant) from the pan and set to one side in a bowl. Put the tomatoes in a food processor or blender and blitz to a rough paste. Cook the onion in the same pan as the aubergine until soft, adding a little oil if needed.

Mince the garlic and chilli together, add to the onion in the pan and cook for 30 seconds.

Add the tomatoes and cook gently for about 15 minutes until the mixture is thickened and rich. Add the aubergine back in, along with the marjoram, and cook for 5 minutes to bring the flavours together. Season to taste with salt and pepper.

To serve, bring a large saucepan of water to the boil and season as for pasta water (see page 125). Heat the ragu gently in a pan next to it. Add the maltagliati to the boiling water and stir to prevent them sticking. As soon as they float to the surface, lift one out and check its doneness – we are looking for a crisp, al dente texture. If your pasta is freshly rolled this could be as fast as 20 seconds. Using a spider, quickly lift the pasta out into the ragu and stir it through. Using a ladle, add a little of the pasta cooking water to the ragu to create a glossy, creamy texture.

Lay out 4 warmed, rimmed plates or pasta bowls and split the ragu and maltagliati among them. Sprinkle generously with the pangrattato and any leftover herbs.

Tagines are a wonderful way of cooking. My sister brought me one back from her honeymoon in Morocco and it spent years sat collecting dust. One day I was stuck for something to cook and decided to give it a go. It was so simple yet the flavours produced inside were a revelation. I don't fully understand the science, but you can't replicate it any other way – casseroles and stew pots just don't have the same effect. This recipe is one of our family favourites, even our 18-month-old son enjoys it at least once a week.

Serves: 4

CARROT, PEA & CARDAMOM TAGINE
with seeded freekeh and flat breads

25ml (1fl oz/5 tsp) extra virgin olive oil

2 onions, sliced

5g (⅛oz/1 tsp) sea salt

5g (⅛oz/2½ tsp) cumin seeds

5g (⅛oz/2½ tsp) coriander seeds, crushed

1 dried red chilli

25g (1oz) organic ginger (see page 58), finely grated

4 cloves of garlic, puréed (see page 145)

12 small shallots, peeled but whole

4 small new potatoes, cut lengthways into quarters

20 baby carrots, trimmed

2g (1 tbsp) saffron

8 cardamom pods

500ml (18fl oz/2 cups) basic stock (see page 62)

150g (5½oz/1 cup) freshly podded peas

50g (1¾oz) sugar snap peas, trimmed and strings removed

15g (½oz/¼ cup) parsley leaves, finely chopped

15g (½oz/generous ½ cup) mint leaves, finely chopped

TO SERVE
seeded freekeh (see page 112)
flat breads (see page 213)

Preheat the oven to (fan) 160°C/180°C/350°F/gas mark 4. Make the seeded freekeh (see page 112) and flat breads (see page 213).

Heat the olive oil gently in a frying pan (skillet), then add the onion and salt and fry for 4 minutes until soft. Add the cumin and coriander seeds and the dried chilli and fry for 1 minute, then add the ginger and garlic. Cook for another 2 minutes and add the shallots and potatoes. Cook for 2 more minutes, then add the carrots, saffron and cardamom pods.

Transfer everything to the tagine and add the stock. Put the lid on the tagine and put it in the oven for 45 minutes. After 30 minutes check the carrots and potatoes. They should be meltingly soft but not broken down. If they are not ready, return to the oven and check every 15 minutes until done. Once done, add the podded peas and return to the oven for 5 minutes.

Remove from the oven and add the sugar snap peas, put the lid on and leave to steam for 30 seconds. Remove the lid and sprinkle the herbs over the top.

Serve the tagine with seeded freekeh and flat breads.

It was my childhood dislike of cauliflower that drove a relentless search for the best possible ways to cook it. In general, I have found the most interesting and satisfying treatments have had an Indian slant.

The slightly bitter edge and the deep sweetness that comes from cooking cauliflower close to burning marries so well with pungent spices. This recipe puts the stem at the heart of the meal and is one of my favourites. Although it takes a little time, it is well worth it. In fact, I'd say that cauliflower is now a contender for one of my favourite vegetables.

Serves: 4

CAULIFLOWER HEARTS
with cauliflower and truffle purée and cauliflower and almond fritters

FOR THE CAULIFLOWER HEARTS
1 very large cauliflower or
  2 medium cauliflowers
rapeseed oil, for frying

FOR THE PURÉES
1 x quantity of kale purée (see
  page 183)
400g (14oz) cauliflower florets
  (reserved from the hearts)
40ml (1½fl oz/8 tsp) extra virgin
  olive oil
sea salt
white truffle oil
water

FOR THE FRITTER FILLING
25 blanched almonds
115g (4oz) cauliflower offcuts from
  the cauliflower hearts (see above)
20ml (4 tsp) rapeseed oil
1g (½ tsp) fenugreek seeds
1g (½ tsp) cumin seeds
small pinch of cayenne pepper
200ml (7fl oz/generous ¾ cup)
  water
0.85g (¼ tsp) agar powder
1.25g (⅓ tsp) iota carrageenan
  powder (or omit the iota
  carrageenan powder and use a
  total of 2g (generous ½ tsp) of
  agar powder)
sea salt

Soak the almonds for the fritters in advance. Place the almonds in a small bowl and cover with water by at least 2cm (¾ inch). Leave for 12 hours, then drain.

Prepare the pickled cauliflower (see page 96) and the kale purée (see page 183).

Cut the stalk and top from the cauliflower, then cut across the cauliflower in half and then cut each half in half again to give 4 discs, each 1–1.5cm (about ½ inch) thick. Using a 7.5cm (3-inch) round cookie cutter, carefully cut out the centre of the cauliflower discs. Reserve the florets and offcuts for the purée and fritters.

Bring 2 litres (3½ pints/8 cups) of water and 30g (1¼oz/1¾ tbsp) of salt to the boil in a large saucepan. Cook the cauliflower hearts for 4–5 minutes until soft but still al dente then shock in ice-cold water (see page 183). Transfer to the fridge.

Preheat the oven to (fan) 160°C/180°C/350°F/gas mark 4.

Toss the cauliflower florets for the purée in the olive oil and a little salt. Place in a baking tin (pan) and roast in the oven for 25 minutes or until golden in colour. Remove from the oven. Weigh the roasted cauliflower and then add 15 per cent of the weight in truffle oil (add 15ml (1 tbsp) of truffle oil for every 100g (3½oz) of cauliflower). Weigh again and calculate 50 per cent of the weight and measure this in water. Add the cauliflower, truffle oil and water to a blender and blend until very smooth, adding a little more water if needed. Taste and adjust the seasoning (see page 13), then chill in the fridge.

Prepare the fritters. Place 8 small, cylindrical moulds on a sheet of baking parchment on a baking tray (sheet). Chop the cauliflower offcuts into 1cm (½-inch) chunks.

Put the rapeseed oil and fenugreek seeds into a frying pan (skillet) and fry gently until they begin to darken but not burn. Add the cumin seeds and cayenne pepper and stir to combine. Add the cauliflower, almonds and measured water and turn down the heat. Stew gently for 15–20 minutes until the cauliflower is completely soft and the water has completely evaporated.

FOR THE BATTER

50g (1¾oz/scant ½ cup) gram flour, plus extra to coat
40g (1½oz/¼ cup) potato flour
0.3g (large pinch) xanthan gum
5g (⅛ oz/1 tsp) caster (superfine) sugar
1g (¼ tsp) quick yeast
1g (scant ¼ tsp) sea salt, finely ground
150ml (5fl oz/⅔ cup) water at room temperature
vegetable oil, for deep-fat frying

TO SERVE

pickled cauliflower (see page 96)
truffle oil
coriander (cilantro) or micro coriander (micro cilantro) leaves

Stir in the agar and iota powders. Bring to the boil, then transfer to a blender. Blend until very smooth, then pass through a fine sieve into a jug. Taste and season well with salt (if the fenugreek tastes bitter then add more salt). Pour it quickly into the prepared moulds. Leave for 30 minutes, then transfer to the fridge and leave for 2 hours.

About an hour before serving, make the batter. Mix all the dry ingredients together in a bowl, then add the water and whisk to form a batter. Leave somewhere warm for an hour. Take the roasted cauliflower purée and the kale purée out of the fridge 1 hour before needed to come to room temperature. Take the pickled cauliflower out of the fridge and drain away all the liquid.

Preheat the oven to (fan) 160°C/180°C/350°F/gas mark 4. Line a small baking tray (sheet) with baking parchment. Prepare your deep-fat fryer (see page 24).

Heat a little rapeseed oil in the bottom of a large frying pan (skillet). Add the cauliflower hearts and fry on a high heat until golden brown. Remove from the pan, put onto the prepared tray and keep warm in the oven.

The curried cauliflower and almond fritters will only keep for 4 minutes when cooked so only do the following once everything else is ready. Remove the fritters from the moulds. Whisk the batter with a fork to knock the bubbles out of it. Toss the fritters in gram flour to coat, then place into the batter mix. Using a fork, lower each fritter into the hot oil. Shake the pan gently to prevent it sticking to the bottom and repeat with each fritter, taking care not to let them stick to each other (you may need to do this in batches). When golden brown, remove and drain on kitchen (paper) towel.

To serve, drizzle a spoonful of the kale purée around the edge of each plate. Put a spoonful of roasted cauliflower and truffle purée in the centre of each plate and drag it with the back of a spoon. Place the cauliflower heart and cauliflower almond fritter on top of the purée. Drizzle a little truffle oil over the top and then add a few coriander (cilantro) leaves. Scatter 8 pieces of pickled cauliflower around and serve it all together while still warm.

THE MAILLARD REACTION

The Maillard reaction is the complex chemical interaction between proteins and sugars in a foodstuff when exposed to a high, direct heat source. Think of the brown bits on roast potatoes, the deep flavour of fried onions, or the texture of crispy cabbage – it is the Maillard reaction that results in the browning of vegetables and leads to a complex satisfying flavour.

No vegetable demonstrates the importance of the Maillard reaction in cooking vegetables as well as the cauliflower. When you boil cauliflower you are dissolving the natural sugars and nutrients into the water, thus making it less sweet and nutritious, as well as breaking down the cell walls and releasing all the sulphurous, cabbage flavours.

Applying a direct, high, heat source, such as sautéing, to completely dry cauliflower, until a deep golden brown colour, encourages the sugars and proteins in the cauliflower to react and create a complex, biscuity flavour that is magical. The key here is colour: you want a deep golden brown on as much of the surface as possible – too light and no magic will have taken place (it will just taste like boiled cauliflower); too dark and it will be burnt because the molecules will have interacted to the point of destruction.

I love the flavour of roasted winter squash. It has a deep, sweet umami (see page 14) and a wonderful colour, it's just a shame about the texture. The more you roast it, the better the flavour, but the more mushy the texture becomes. Slicing it very finely and setting it in a terrine is my solution to this problem as you get the soft bite of the multiple layers combined with the wonderful depth of flavour that comes from slow cooking in the oven. This recipe will make more terrine than you need, but you can either double up on the portions or save it for an elegant lunch with bread and a nice green salad.

Serves: 4

PRESSED WINTER SQUASH
with cavolo nero, smoked hazelnut milk and rye grain

FOR THE RYE GRAIN

80g (2¾oz/½ cup) rye grain
pinch of salt
1 x quantity of smoked hazelnut
    milk (see page 221)

FOR THE PRESSED SQUASH

300g (10½oz) peeled and
    deseeded butternut squash
600g (1lb 5oz) peeled and
    deseeded muscat de provence
    squash
10g (¼oz/1¾ tsp) sea salt
50g (1¾oz/¼ cup) caster
    (superfine) sugar
1 clove of garlic, puréed (see page
    145)
2.5g (3 tsp) sage leaves, sliced
1.5g (¾ tsp) grated lemon zest
4g (1¼ tsp) agar powder
drizzle of hazelnut oil

FOR THE PICKLED SQUASH

12 slices of butternut squash
50ml (2fl oz/scant ¼ cup) cider
    vinegar
50g (1¾oz/¼ cup) caster
    (superfine) sugar
150ml (5fl oz/⅔ cup) water
5g (⅛oz/1 tsp) sea salt

Put the rye grain into a bowl and completely cover in cold water. Soak for at least 4 hours. When soaked, drain and rinse and put into a small saucepan, cover with water and add a pinch of salt. Boil gently for about 30 minutes until the grain is soft but with a "pop". Drain and set aside.

Prepare the smoked hazelnut milk (see page 221). Prepare the cavolo nero purée (see page 183). Line a 900g (2lb) loaf tin (pan) with baking parchment.

Cut 12 x 1mm thin, round slices of butternut from the top of the butternut squash for the pickled squash and set aside. Cut the rest of the butternut squash into very thin slices on a mandolin. Do the same for the muscat squash. Weigh out the correct amount of each squash and place in a large bowl, reserving the rest of the squash for the purée. Mix the salt and sugar together and mix with the squash slices. Set aside for 30 minutes.

Make the pickled squash. Place the vinegar, sugar, water and salt in a saucepan and heat until boiling. Add the 12 slices of butternut squash and simmer for 3–5 minutes until soft, then remove from the heat and allow to cool in the liquid.

Make the pressed squash. Mix together the garlic, sage and lemon zest, then add to the muscat and butternut squash. Sprinkle the agar over the top and mix to combine. Preheat the oven to (fan) 160°C/180°C/350°F/gas mark 4.

Layer the squash slices in the prepared loaf tin (pan), pressing down to ensure even density. Once all the squash is in, push down again to compact. Cover in a sheet of baking parchment and then wrap very tightly in foil to seal. Bake in the oven for 45–60 minutes.

While the terrine is cooking, make the squash purée. Place a piece of baking parchment 45cm (18 inches) long on a baking tray (sheet). Place the squash in the middle, add the olive oil and salt, then roll up the baking parchment to form a sealed parcel. Bake in the oven for 25 minutes until the squash is soft. Remove from the oven, allow to cool for 5 minutes, then transfer the contents to a blender along with the hazelnut oil. Blend until very smooth and then taste and adjust the seasoning if necessary (see page 13). Set aside.

FOR THE PURÉES

5 tbsp cavolo nero purée (see page 183)

250g (9oz) squash (reserved from the offcuts from the terrine, cut into equal-sized chunks)

10ml (2tsp) extra virgin olive oil

1g (scant ¼ tsp) sea salt

15ml (1 tbsp) hazelnut oil

FOR THE GARNISH

4 cavolo nero leaves, stems removed

hazelnut oil, to drizzle

Stick a cocktail stick through the terrine foil into the squash to test if it is done. When it is ready it should meet no resistance. If you feel it click through the layers, put it back into the oven in 10-minute bursts until ready. When ready, remove from the oven and, using another loaf tin (pan) or similar, press down on the terrine to compress the squash. Leave the empty tin (pan) in place and fill it with a full jam jar or similar weight. Leave on a cooling rack until cold, then remove the weights and put the terrine into the fridge for 1 hour.

When chilled, remove from the fridge and remove the foil. Turn the tin (pan) out, remove the paper liner and trim the edges to a neat rectangle. Cut widthways into neat slices about 1.5cm (½ inch) across. Line a baking tray (sheet) with baking parchment and arrange the 4 pressed squash slices on it. Put into the oven for 10 minutes to reheat.

Take each of the 12 slices of pickled squash and cut from the centre straight out to one edge. Lift one cut side over the other and twist it round to form a cone. Put these to one side for garnish.

Put the cavolo nero purée into a small saucepan with 1 tsp of water and heat through gently. At the same time, put the rye grain in a small saucepan and just cover with the smoked hazelnut milk. Bring to a simmer and cook gently to thicken to a risotto consistency.

Meanwhile, blanch the cavolo nero leaves for 3 minutes, then shock in ice-cold water (see page 183).

Remove the pressed squash from the oven and drizzle each piece with hazelnut oil to give it a glossy sheen. Place 1 slice on each of 4 plates. Lay 1 strip of blanched cavolo nero leaf next to each slice and place a spoonful of the cavolo nero purée on top. Fold it over to contain the purée and then add a pile of the hazelnut rye mix next to it and add 2 tablespoons of squash purée. Arrange 3 pickled squash cones around the plate and drizzle a little hazelnut oil over the top. Serve immediately.

| PURÉES |

I make a lot of purées ... and I mean a lot of purées. They are a great way to use offcuts of vegetables and they bring a lovely, vibrant colour and a creamy texture that can help to lift a dish from a few nice things on a plate to a true eating experience.

ASPARAGUS & HERB PURÉE

Makes: 4 portions

250g (9oz) asparagus
75ml (2¾fl oz/⅓ cup) extra virgin olive oil
100g (3½oz) onion, sliced
25g (1oz/scant 1 cup) spinach
5g (⅛oz/2 tbsp) chopped parsley leaves
2g (2 tsp) tarragon leaves
200ml (7fl oz/generous ¾ cup) cold water
sea salt

Cut the asparagus stems into 5mm (¼-inch) slices, discarding the tough, woody ends.

Heat 25ml (1fl oz/5 tsp) of the olive oil in a large saucepan and add the onion. Simmer gently until the onion is beginning to soften, then add the asparagus. Cook until soft but still green, then add the spinach, parsley and tarragon. Stir and cook until the spinach leaves have just wilted.

Transfer to a blender, add the measured water and remaining olive oil and blend until the purée is completely smooth. Season to taste (see page 13). Pass through a sieve and put straight into a container, covered with cling film (plastic wrap) in contact with the purée, to cool quickly.

This will keep in the fridge for up to 2 days.

CHERVIL PURÉE

Makes: 4 portions

50g (1¾oz/generous ¾ cup) chervil leaves
50g (1¾oz /generous ¾ cup) parsley leaves
105ml (3½fl oz/scant ½ cup) extra virgin olive oil
75g (2¾oz) shallots, sliced
100g (3½oz/3⅓ cups) spinach
10ml (2 tsp) black truffle oil
sea salt

Put a small metal baking tin (pan) in the freezer to chill. Blanch the chervil and parsley for about 90 seconds, until a vibrant green colour, then shock in ice-cold water (see page 183). Remove the herbs from the water and squeeze dry. Chop roughly and set aside.

Heat 30ml (1fl oz/2 tbsp) of the olive oil in a frying pan (skillet) and add the shallots. Cook until just soft, then add the spinach. Cook briefly until wilted, then remove from the heat.

Put the shallots and spinach into a blender along with the blanched herbs and remaining olive oil. Blend for at least 4 minutes until silky smooth (you may need to add a little water). Add the truffle oil and season with salt to taste (see page 13). Remove the baking tin (pan) from the freezer and pour the herb purée onto it. Place a sheet of cling film (plastic wrap) tightly against the surface of the purée and refrigerate.

This will keep in the fridge for up to 2 days.

PARSNIP & SHALLOT PURÉE

Makes: 4 portions

25g (1oz/scant ¼ cup) smoked hazelnuts (see page 114)
20ml (4 tsp) extra virgin olive oil
75g (2¾oz) banana shallots, sliced
225g (8oz) parsnips, peeled, trimmed and cut into
    2mm (¹⁄₁₆ inch) slices
250ml (8½fl oz/1 cup) water
15ml (1 tbsp) hazelnut oil

Make the smoked hazelnuts (see page 114).

Heat the olive oil in a large saucepan until just hot, then add
the shallots. Cook gently until just soft, then add the parsnip.
Cook gently for 2 minutes, then add the water and simmer
for 15–20 minutes until soft.

Transfer the shallot and parsnip mix into a blender and add
the hazelnut oil and smoked hazelnuts. Process until very
smooth, adding just a little water if needed, to make a thick,
silky purée.

This will keep in the fridge for up to 3 days.

BROAD BEAN
(FAVA BEAN) PURÉE

Makes: 4 portions

50g (1¾oz/⅓ cup) split dried broad beans (fava beans)
25ml (1fl oz/5 tsp) extra virgin olive oil
2 cloves of garlic, thinly sliced
75ml (2¾fl oz/⅓ cup) water
sea salt
cayenne pepper

Put the dried broad beans (fava beans) into a small bowl
and cover with cold water by at least 2cm (¾ inch). Soak
for at least 4 hours or ideally overnight. Strain and rinse in
cold water.

Put the beans into a small saucepan and add 500ml (18fl oz/
2 cups) of cold water. Bring to the boil and simmer very gently
until the beans are cooked but not breaking up.

Put the olive oil into a small saucepan and heat gently. Add
the garlic and cook until soft but not coloured. Add the
broad beans (fava beans) and measured water and bring to
the boil. As soon as it boils, transfer to a blender and blend
until smooth. Season with salt and cayenne pepper to taste
(see page 13).

This will keep in the fridge for up to 3 days.

CARTOUCHE

*Sometimes you want to cover something in a saucepan to slow
down the evaporation of liquids and aromatic compounds,
but a lid will be too efficient at the job. Using a cartouche is
a wonderful way of keeping a succulent stewed texture but
allowing a little liquid to evaporate naturally. It is simply a
round piece of baking parchment the size of the saucepan you
are using, with a small hole in the middle, which is pushed
down on top of the ingredients being cooked.*

KALE PURÉE

Makes: 4 portions

100g (3½oz) kale, stems removed
20ml (4 tsp) extra virgin olive oil
25–75ml (1–2¾fl oz/5 tsp–⅓ cup) water
sea salt

Blanch the kale and then shock in ice-cold water (see box, below). Remove from the water and squeeze out any liquid. Chop the kale roughly, then put in a blender with the olive oil and a little water, starting with 25ml (1fl oz/5 tsp).

Blend to a very smooth purée, adding a little more water if needed. Pass through a sieve and season with salt to taste (see page 13).

This will keep in the fridge for up to 3 days.

CAVOLO NERO PURÉE

Makes: 4 portions

100g (3½oz) cavolo nero leaves, stems removed
1 clove of garlic
30ml (1fl oz/2 tbsp) extra virgin olive oil
sea salt

Blanch the cavolo nero and garlic for 3 minutes, then shock in ice-cold water (see box, opposite). Remove from the water and squeeze out any excess liquid to make a ball. Chop roughly, then put in a blender. Add the olive oil and process to a coarse paste. Season to taste with salt (see page 13).

This will keep in the fridge for up to 3 days.

SUNFLOWER SEED PURÉE

Makes: 4 portions

200g (7oz/1½ cups) sunflower seeds
20g (¾oz/1⅔ tbsp) caster (superfine) sugar
20ml (4 tsp) sunflower oil
200ml (7fl oz/generous ¾ cup) water
sea salt
cayenne pepper

Preheat the oven to (fan) 160°C/180°C/350°F/gas mark 4.

Put the sunflower seeds on a baking tray (sheet) and bake in the oven for 10 minutes until a dark brown colour. Transfer the seeds to a blender with the sugar, oil and water and blend until very smooth. Taste and season with salt and cayenne pepper (see page 13).

This will keep in the fridge for up to 3 days.

BLANCHING AND SHOCKING GREEN VEGETABLES

Keeping your green vegetables green is an important skill to master. It is relatively simple, you just need to remember a few principles:

1. *Have your water at boiling point when you add your vegetables.*
2. *You need a lot of water, so when your greens are added the water doesn't stop boiling and they cook as quickly as possible.*
3. *Add 1.5 per cent of salt to the volume of your water, so for 4 litres (7 pints/16 cups) of water add 60g (2oz/3½ tbsp) of salt (any kind of salt).*
4. *Have a lot of ice-cold water to plunge your greens into once cooked, so the cooking stops instantly and their temperature drops as quickly as possible.*
5. *Don't leave your greens in the cold water once chilled. As soon as they are cold, remove them from the water.*
6. *Keep your blanched greens away from any source of acid until ready to serve or you will risk having a grey/yellow mess just when you want them to look their best.*

DESSERTS

This has become something of a classic at the restaurant, it is so simple to look at, the flavours so familiar, but nothing can prepare you for the intensity and clarity of the flavours. Using as few ingredients as possible in each element allows the purity of the ingredients to shine through – the peanuts taste purely of peanuts, the chocolate and caramel exactly of that. Just remember that the sorbet and the tart need four to five hours to set.

Serves: 8

CHOCOLATE SALTED CARAMEL TART
with peanut butter sorbet

FOR THE SORBET

70g (2½oz/⅓ cup) caster (superfine) sugar
0.5g (scant ¼ tsp) xanthan gum
175ml (6fl oz/¾ cup) cold water
175ml (6fl oz/¾ cup) glucose syrup
150g (5½oz) unsweetened crunchy peanut butter
25ml (1fl oz/5 tsp) brandy

FOR THE TART BASE

90g (3oz/¾ cup) plain (all-purpose) flour
10g (¼oz/1¼ tbsp) cornflour (cornstarch)
20g (¾oz/1⅔ tbsp) caster (superfine) sugar
pinch of salt
30ml (1fl oz/2 tbsp) extra virgin olive oil
20ml (4 tsp) cold water
25g (1oz) dark chocolate, 53% cocoa solids

FOR THE TART FILLING

400g (14oz) dark chocolate, 53% cocoa solids, finely chopped or coarsely grated
7g (¼oz/1¼ tsp) sea salt
125g (4½oz/⅔ cup) caster (superfine) sugar
500ml (10fl oz/1¼ cups) cold water

To serve

4 tsp cocoa nibs

Make the sorbet first. Mix the sugar and xanthan together. Place the measured water in a large saucepan, then whisk in the sugar and xanthan. Add the glucose syrup and peanut butter and bring to the boil. Immediately remove from the heat and add the brandy. Allow the sorbet to cool slightly, then put into an ice-cream machine and follow the manufacturer's instructions before freezing. Or see making sorbets by hand on page 199.

Preheat the oven to (fan) 160°C/180°C/350°F/gas mark 4.

Mix all the ingredients for the tart base together, except for the dark chocolate, in a large bowl to form a dough. Place the dough between 2 sheets of baking parchment and roll it out until 1mm thick (very thin). Refrigerate for 30 minutes.

Put the dough on a large baking tray (sheet), leaving the top sheet of baking parchment on, and bake for 15–25 minutes until just crisp. Remove from the oven and remove the baking parchment. While still hot, place the base of a 21cm (8-inch) springform cake tin (pan) onto the pastry and cut round it. Return the base to the springform tin (pan) and line with baking parchment. Fit the cut pastry base inside. Place the dark chocolate for the tart base in a bain-marie (see box, below) and melt gently. Spread evenly over the pastry base.

Make the tart filling. Place the chocolate and salt in an electric mixer fitted with a whisk attachment. Put the sugar into a small, heavy-based saucepan and gently melt until it becomes a dark caramel. Add the water and simmer until the sugar has melted.

Weigh out 250g (9oz) of the boiling caramel and pour over the chocolate and salt in the electric mixer. Whisk on the lowest speed until the temperature has reduced to 27°C/80°F. Pour the mix onto the base and put in the fridge for 4–5 hours to set.

Remove the chocolate tart from the fridge and from the tin (pan) – use a blowtorch to gently heat the outside if necessary. Cut into slices and place 1 slice on each plate. Place 1 tsp of cocoa nibs next to the tart and top with a quenelle of sorbet.

BAIN-MARIE

Make a bain-marie, or water bath, by setting a heatproof bowl over a small saucepan filled with 2cm (¾ inch) of boiling water. Turn the heat down so the water is just simmering and add the ingredient you wish to melt to the heatproof bowl.

This is a super simple, classic chocolate mousse. Because it is so straightforward, it will taste of the chocolate you use, so try and use the best you can find and definitely only use real chocolate made from beans and sugar. Avoid anything labelled 'cooking chocolate' or containing any fats other than cocoa butter. Pair with whatever takes your fancy; a little peppery olive oil, some fresh cherries or a handful of roasted nuts would work well.

Serves: 4 (large servings)

CHOCOLATE MOUSSE

200g (7oz) aquafaba (chilled) (see page 36)
30g (1¼oz/2½ tbsp) caster (superfine) sugar
2g (⅓ tsp) fine sea salt
200g (7oz) dark chocolate (70% cocoa solids), cut into fine pieces
150g (5½oz) boiling water

Put the aquafaba into a mixing bowl and whisk until it forms stiff peaks. Add the sugar and salt a little at a time and continue to whisk until it holds glossy stiff peaks.

Put the chocolate into a large mixing bowl. Pour the boiling water on top and stir to combine and emulsify. If the chocolate isn't completely melted, then warm it gently on a bain marie or in a microwave in short bursts until it is melted and glossy.

Make sure your whipped aquafaba is still holding stiff peaks (whisking it again if not) and gently fold a third into the chocolate mix. Add another third of the mix and carefully fold this in, then add the remaining third and gently fold in until just combined. Pour into a clean container, cover with a lid and put in the fridge for 8 hours or overnight.

Scoop generously onto 4 plates or into glasses and serve with your chosen toppings.

COCOA PERCENTAGES

If you want to use a chocolate that has a different cocoa percentage than specified in this recipe, then you will need to adjust the quantities of chocolate used (the recipe here is for 70% chocolate – anything in that region will work just fine). If you want to use chocolate in the 50% region, multiply the amount by 1.5 (so for 100g of 70%, add 150g of 50%). For chocolate in the 30% region, try multiplying by 2.5 (for 100g of 70%, add 250g of 30%) but this will depend a little on what the bulk of that chocolate is made up from (sugar, oats, nuts, milks etc.).

You've probably come across strawberries with basil and black pepper before, it's such a good combination that it no longer appears that innovative. This dish takes flavours that normally form a savoury salad and ups the sweetness to balance the strawberries and therefore make a lovely dessert instead. This recipe makes 8 parfaits, but they keep well in the freezer. Allow up to 8 hours for the parfait to set and 4 hours for the strawberries to macerate.

Serves: 4

MACERATED STRAWBERRIES
with pine nut parfait and thyme meringues

FOR THE PARFAIT
50g (1¾oz/⅓ cup) pine nuts
75g (2¾oz/½ cup) cashew nuts
15ml (3 tsp) lemon juice
0.35g (scant ¼ tsp) lemon zest
75ml (2¾fl oz/⅓ cup) water
125g (4½oz/⅔ cup) caster (superfine) sugar
25ml (1fl oz/5 tsp) glucose syrup
4g (¾ tsp) sea salt
1g (⅓ tsp) xanthan gum
150g (5½oz/⅔ cup) fridge-cold coconut cream
50ml (2fl oz/scant ¼ cup) aquafaba (see page 36)
50g (1¾oz/¼ cup) caster (superfine) sugar

FOR THE MERINGUES
50ml (2fl oz/scant ¼ cup) aquafaba (see page 36)
1g (scant ¼ tsp) sea salt
50g (1¾oz/¼ cup) caster (superfine) sugar
2g (2½ tsp) thyme leaves
freshly ground black pepper

FOR THE STRAWBERRIES
200g (7oz) ripe strawberries
20g (¾oz/1⅔ tbsp) caster (superfine) sugar
10ml (2 tsp) lemon juice
4 tbsp good, peppery olive oil

FOR DECORATION
24 small basil leaves
handful of toasted pine nuts

Preheat the oven to (fan) 160°C/180°C/350°F/gas mark 4. Prepare 8 x 4cm (1½-inch) moulds. Wrap the bases in cling film (plastic wrap) and place on a baking tray (sheet). Make the parfait. Put the pine nuts and cashews onto a baking tray (sheet) and toast in the oven for 5 minutes. Add to a blender with the lemon juice and zest, the water, sugar, glucose syrup, salt and xanthan. Blend until very smooth, then pass through a sieve into a mixing bowl. Place in the fridge, covered with cling film (plastic wrap), to firm up for 20 minutes.

Put the coconut cream into a bowl and, using a wire whisk, whisk until it forms stiff peaks. Add a third of the coconut cream to the pine nut mix and stir it in. Add a further third and fold it in gently, then add the remaining third and fold it in carefully. Return the mix to the fridge while you prepare the aquafaba.

Put the aquafaba for the parfait into a clean bowl and whisk to soft peaks. Add the sugar 2 tbsp at a time and whisk until all the sugar is incorporated and it is glossy and holds stiff peaks. Add a third of the mix to the pine nut mix and stir it in. Add a further third and fold it in, then add the last third and fold it in. Spoon the parfait into your moulds and freeze for 4–8 hours.

Make the meringues. Ideally use a dehydrator set to 60°C/140°F. If using the oven, preheat to its lowest setting. Line a dehydrator tray or baking tray (sheet) with baking parchment. Put the aquafaba and salt into a clean mixing bowl and whisk to form stiff peaks. Add the sugar 1 tbsp at a time and whisk in before adding more. Continue until all the sugar is incorporated and you have stiff peaks. Fold the thyme leaves in and transfer to a piping bag. Pipe 1cm (½-inch) meringues onto the tray. Grind black pepper over the top and bake in the dehydrator or oven for 4–8 hours or until dry and crisp all the way through. Quarter the strawberries, put into a bowl and toss in the sugar and lemon juice. Cover the bowl with cling film (plastic wrap) and put into the fridge for 4 hours.

When ready, spoon most of the macerated strawberries out of their liquid (keeping some for garnish) onto kitchen (paper) towel to dry. In a small bowl, mix 4 tablespoons of the strawberry juice with the olive oil. Remove 4 parfaits from the freezer and warm in your hands until the parfait comes loose. Place 1 parfait on each of 4 dessert plates and pile a quarter of the macerated strawberries next to it. Add about 6 small basil leaves and dress the strawberries with the strawberry and olive oil mix. Scatter a few pine nuts on top and add 4–5 meringues to each plate. Serve immediately.

Peaches and prosecco are at the heart of a Bellini cocktail. However, it is a little sickly sweet for my taste. This recipe burns the sugars in the peach to give a more complex experience and uses a touch of lemon thyme to add a herbaceous lemony tinge. You need four hours for the sorbet to set and at least four hours for the peaches to macerate.

Serves: 4

BURNT PEACHES
with prosecco sorbet and almond biscotti

FOR THE PEACHES
4 yellow-fleshed peaches, ripe but
　firm, halved and stones removed
caster (superfine) sugar
4 sprigs of lemon thyme

FOR THE SORBET
225g (8oz/1⅛ cups) caster
　(superfine) sugar
225ml (7½fl oz/scant 1 cup) water
300ml (10floz/1¼ cups) prosecco
90ml (3¼fl oz/generous ⅓ cup)
　lemon juice

FOR THE BISCOTTI
75g (2¾oz/½ cup) almonds
100g (3½oz/¾ cup) plain
　(all-purpose) flour
100g (3½oz/½ cup) caster
　(superfine) sugar
2.5g (½ tsp) baking powder
twist of grated nutmeg
zest of ½ lemon
50ml (2fl oz/scant ¼ cup) cold
　water

FOR DECORATION
4 sprigs of lemon thyme leaves,
　picked

Slice a little off the back of the peaches to give a flat surface. Weigh the peaches and measure 20 per cent of their weight in sugar (for 500g (1lb 2oz) of peaches weigh 100g (3½oz/½ cup) of sugar). Put the peaches and sugar into a bowl and mix well. Leave for at least 4 hours, or overnight in the fridge.

Make the sorbet. Put the sugar and water into a small lidded saucepan and heat until the sugar dissolves, ideally without boiling. Remove from the heat and allow to cool completely, then mix in the prosecco and lemon juice. If using an ice-cream maker, follow the manufacturer's instructions then store in the freezer. Otherwise see making sorbets by hand on page 199.

Make the biscotti. Preheat the oven to (fan) 160°C/180°C/350°F/gas mark 4. Line a large baking tray (sheet) with non-stick baking parchment. In a blender, process half the almonds until coarsely crushed then mix with the whole almonds and the rest of the ingredients except the water. Add the water and bring together into a dough. Roll the dough into a log 4cm (1½ inches) in diameter. Place the log on the baking tray (sheet) and bake in the oven for 25 minutes or until light brown. Remove from the oven, allow to cool, then slice into 1cm (½-inch) slices.

Re-line the baking tray (sheet) and lay the biscotti out. Turn the oven down to (fan) 140°C/160°C/310°F/gas mark 2½ and put the biscotti back into the oven for 10–15 minutes. Remove from the oven and allow to cool completely – they should be hard and crunchy once cool. Place 3 biscotti in a food processor and pulse to coarse crumbs.

Remove the peaches from their macerating liquid and pat dry with kitchen (paper) towel. Line a large frying pan (skillet) with non-stick baking parchment and heat until searing hot. Add the peaches, cut side down, along with the lemon thyme. Cook until completely caramelized and burnt in appearance. Flip over and repeat on the other side. Remove from the heat and place 2 slices, cut side up, on each of 4 dessert plates.

Add a little pile of biscotti to each plate, scoop a large ball of sorbet on top, and add 2 biscotti. Scatter the thyme leaves over the top and serve straight away.

This dessert is really a fancy Bakewell tart. I didn't mean to create it that way; it was only when I put it together on the plate that it clicked. I wanted to make a beautiful almond and olive oil slice using artisan techniques and I came up with this frangipane-like creation that has a really moreish quality. It's great with a cup of coffee in the morning, but to form a dessert it needed something to cut through it and raspberries were the obvious choice. It turns out it was obvious because it is one of the classic English desserts. So much for originality!

Serves: 8

ALMOND SPONGE
with raspberry and vodka sorbet

FOR THE GRAM FLOUR FERMENT
60g (2oz/½ cup) gram flour
90ml (3¼fl oz/generous ⅓ cup)
    water

FOR THE SORBET
450g (1lb/3⅔ cups) raspberries
    (fresh or frozen)
150g (5½oz/¾ cup) caster
    (superfine) sugar
100ml (3½fl oz/scant ½ cup)
    glucose syrup
200ml (7fl oz/generous ¾ cup)
    water
50ml (2fl oz/scant ¼ cup) vodka
1g (⅓ tsp) xanthan gum

FOR THE SPONGE
125g (4½oz/1 cup) plain (all-
    purpose) flour
75g (2¾oz/⅔ cup) ground almonds
5g (⅛ oz/1 tsp) baking powder
150g (5½oz) gram flour ferment
    (see above)
200g (7oz/1 cup) caster (superfine)
    sugar
3ml (generous ½ tsp) almond
    extract
3g (½ tsp) sea salt
125ml (4fl oz/½ cup) extra virgin
    olive oil
15g (½oz/2½ tbsp) flaked almonds

FOR DECORATION
16 toasted blanched almonds

First make the gram flour ferment as it needs 24 hours to ferment. Sieve the gram flour, then put it into a small clean jar and add the water. Mix together to form a smooth paste. Cover the jar with a piece of muslin (cheesecloth) or kitchen (paper) towel and fasten using string or an elastic band. Leave in a warm place (23–26°C/73–79°F) for a minimum of 8 hours, an optimum of 24 hours, and a maximum of 48 hours.

Make the sorbet in advance so it can set. Put the raspberries, sugar, glucose syrup and water in a saucepan and cover with a lid. Gently bring to the boil and simmer, stirring occasionally, for about 5 minutes. Transfer to a blender with the vodka and xanthan and blend until smooth. Sieve into a bowl and allow to cool. Transfer to an ice-cream maker and follow the manufacturer's instructions, then store in the freezer. Otherwise see making sorbets by hand on page 199.

When ready to make the cake, check the gram flour ferment – the mix should appear bubbly. Preheat the oven to (fan) 140°C/160°C/310°F/gas mark 2½. Grease and line a 21cm (8-inch) springform cake tin (pan) with baking parchment.

Mix the flour, ground almonds and baking powder together in a bowl. Put the meaured gram flour ferment, sugar, almond extract and salt together in another bowl and whisk until the sugar has dissolved. Slowly add the oil to emulsify. If it starts to split add 1 tbsp of the flour mix. Once all the oil is incorporated, add the flour in 3 batches and stir gently until mixed. Transfer to the prepared cake tin (pan) and scatter the flaked almonds over the top. Bake in the oven for 40 minutes. When cooked it should be golden brown and the middle should no longer wobble.

Remove the tin (pan) and let the cake cool completely on a wire rack. Chop the toasted almonds into a coarse crumb. Cut 8 slices of almond cake and place a slice on each of 8 dessert plates. Place a little pile of chopped almonds next to each slice of cake and top with a scoop of sorbet. Serve before the sorbet melts.

This frozen olive oil dessert is a miracle. It is rich, buttery and moreish. Even if you don't like pineapple it is worth making the semi-freddo. Sometimes I serve it with a tomato salad as a starter, sometimes with strawberries. Pineapple and anise flavours are a match made in heaven, and the olive oil's richness is the perfect accompaniment.

Serves: 4

SPICED PINEAPPLE
with candied fennel and olive oil semi-freddo

FOR THE SEMI-FREDDO
175g (6¼oz/generous ¾ cup) caster (superfine) sugar
5g (⅛oz/2 tsp) soy lecithin
1g (⅓ tsp) xanthan gum
3g (½ tsp) sea salt
150ml (5fl oz/⅔ cup) water
15ml (1 tbsp) pernod (or vodka)
125ml (4fl oz/½ cup) grassy Sicilian olive oil

FOR THE FENNEL
50g (1¾oz/¼ cup) caster (superfine) sugar
1 star anise
150ml (5fl oz/⅔ cup) water
2 vanilla pods, cut in half and seeds scraped
50ml (2fl oz/scant ¼ cup) lemon juice
1 head fennel, stalk and outer layers removed

FOR THE POACHED PINEAPPLE
1 large pineapple
300ml (10fl oz/1¼ cups) water
100g (3½oz/½ cup) caster (superfine) sugar
1 star anise

FOR DECORATION
pineapple (reserved from above)
candled fennel seeds (see page 114)
20g (¾oz/scant 1 cup) basil leaves, shredded
10g (¼oz/generous ⅓ cup) mint leaves, finely sliced

Make the semi-freddo a day before serving so it can set. Mix the sugar, soy lecithin, xanthan and salt together in a bowl. Put the water in a saucepan and whisk in the sugar mix, bit by bit. Gently heat without boiling and stir until the sugar dissolves. Remove from the heat, cover with a lid and leave to cool completely. Transfer to a blender with the pernod and turn on just enough to form a vortex. Slowly pour in the olive oil as if making an aioli (see page 36). Keep adding the oil very slowly to emulsify. When all the mix has been incorporated put into an ice-cream maker and follow the manufacturer's instructions. (Or put in the freezer and whisk by hand every 30 minutes until a softly whipped cream consistency.) Freeze in a pre-chilled container lined with cling film (plastic wrap) for at least 4 hours.

Prepare the fennel at least 4 hours before serving. Put the sugar, star anise and measured water into a small saucepan and heat gently until the sugar dissolves. Add the vanilla seeds and lemon juice, then put in the fridge to chill until icy cold. Cut across the base of the fennel to reveal a flat, wide area, then cut into paper-thin wafers on a mandolin. Put the fennel slices into the prepared sugar syrup and leave for 4 hours.

Make the candied fennel seeds (see page 114).

Remove the pineapple skin then cut the flesh into quarters lengthways. Cut out the core and cut 2 of the quarters into 2 neat large batons, giving 4 batons in total. Reserve the remaining pineapple for the garnish. Put the water in a jug. Put the sugar in a small heavy-bottomed saucepan over a medium heat and melt the sugar, stirring, until a deep caramel colour. Standing back, confidently pour the water onto the caramel (it will violently spit). Add the star anise and simmer until the sugar has dissolved. Put the pineapple batons into the caramel stock and simmer gently for 15 minutes, then remove from the heat and leave to cool completely. Remove the pineapple from the caramel and trim into sharp, square-edged, perfect batons, before returning to the caramel.

Shave paper-thin slices of pineapple from the reserved pineapple on a mandolin until you have 1 tablespoon per portion. Dry on kitchen (paper) towel. Place the poached pineapple and 4 handfuls of the sweet vanilla fennel on kitchen (paper) towel to dry.

Place 1 poached pineapple baton on each of 4 dessert plates. Arrange a little of the fennel salad, shaved pineapple, basil and mint on top and add a pinch of candied fennel seeds. Remove the semifreddo from the freezer, turn it out and cut into chunks. Place 3 semifreddo chunks next to the baton and arrange the fennel, pineapple, basil and mint next to it. Drizzle lightly with the vanilla syrup from the fennel and serve.

I tend not to think of making desserts as a separate way of cooking with a different set of ingredients. I view it more as cooking with ingredients that have a higher sugar content and so need higher sugar content garnishes to balance the plate. As a result, I don't view any ingredient as off limits so long as it benefits from a sweet touch. Here olive oil and rosemary slip effortlessly into a dessert context.

Serves: 4–8

CHOCOLATE OLIVE OIL POT
with rosemary soil and raspberry sorbet

FOR THE CHOCOLATE POTS
200g (7oz) dark chocolate, 53–55% cocoa solids, coarsely grated
50ml (2fl oz/scant ¼ cup) extra virgin olive oil
2g (⅓ tsp) sea salt
165ml (5½fl oz/⅔ cup) boiling water

FOR THE SORBET
450g (1lb/3⅔ cups) raspberries (fresh or frozen)
150g (5½oz/¾ cup) caster (superfine) sugar
100ml (3½fl oz/scant ½ cup) glucose syrup
200ml (7fl oz/generous ¾ cup) water
25ml (1fl oz/5 tsp) red wine vinegar
1g (⅓ tsp) xanthan gum

FOR THE ROSEMARY SOIL
50g (1¾oz/¼ cup) caster (superfine) sugar
25ml (1fl oz/5 tsp) water
50g (1¾oz) dark chocolate, 53–55% cocoa solids, coarsely grated
2g (4 tsp) rosemary leaves, finely chopped

FOR DECORATION
8–16 raspberries

First make the chocolate pots as they need 4 hours to set. Put the chocolate into the bowl of an electric mixer (or a heatproof mixing bowl) and add the olive oil and salt, then add the boiling water, which should melt the chocolate. If the chocolate doesn't melt completely, set the bowl briefly over a bain-marie (see page 186) to fully melt. Gently whisk the chocolate until it cools to 27°C/80°F or is cool to the touch. You can speed this up by placing the bowl in a larger bowl filled with cold water. When the chocolate is at the correct temperature, pour the mix into 4 to 8 pots or tea cups and put into the fridge for 4 hours to set.

Next make the raspberry sorbet. Put the raspberries, sugar, glucose syrup and measured water into a lidded saucepan. Gently bring to the boil and simmer, stirring occasionally, for about 5 minutes. Transfer the raspberry mix to a blender with the red wine vinegar and xanthan and blend until completely smooth. Sieve into a bowl and allow to cool completely. Transfer to an ice-cream maker and follow the manufacturer's instructions then store in the freezer. Otherwise see making sorbets by hand (below).

Make the rosemary soil. Put the sugar and water into a small saucepan and heat gently until it reaches 137°C/278°F. Remove from the heat, add the chocolate and rosemary and stir vigorously until the sugar crystallizes then leave to cool.

Place 1 chocolate pot on each of 4 dessert plates. Sprinkle a little of the rosemary soil onto the chocolate pot and add a pile next to the pot. Top with a scoop of sorbet, add a couple of raspberries and serve straight away.

MAKING SORBETS BY HAND

If not using an ice-cream maker, pour the sorbet mix into a 2-litre (3½-pint) container and put into the freezer. After 2 hours whisk vigorously to break up the ice crystals. Repeat every 45 minutes for up to 6 hours (depending on your freezer) until the mix is frozen through and as free from crystals as possible. Sorbets will keep in the freezer for up to 1 month.

A semifreddo is one of life's great frozen desserts, easy to make and serve without any special equipment, and luxurious and impressive at the table. I've made this version with pistachios but you could easily use almost any other nut; almonds, pine nuts and macadamias spring to mind most readily. You could also mix in any fruit that you have to hand, folding in a few handfuls before freezing.

Serves: 4

POACHED PEARS
with pistachio semifreddo

FOR THE PISTACHIO MIX
160g (5¾oz) shelled, unsalted pistachios, plus 60g (2oz) pistachios for stirring through the mix
180ml (6fl oz/¾ cup) water
zest of ½ lemon
1 tbsp lemon juice
seeds scraped from 2 vanilla pods
100g (3½oz/½ cup) caster (superfine) sugar

FOR THE MERINGUE MIX
100g (3½oz) aquafaba (see page 36)
100g (3½oz/½ cup) caster (superfine) sugar

FOR THE POACHED PEARS
4 ripe, firm Williams pears
250ml (8½fl oz/1 cup) white wine
125ml (4fl oz/½ cup) cold water
125g (4½oz/⅔ cup) caster (superfine) sugar
2g (1 tsp) cardamom pods
0.2g (pinch) saffron

Line a small (400g/14oz) loaf tin (pan) with baking parchment and set to one side.

Put all the ingredients for the pistachio mix (setting aside the extra 60g/2oz pistachios) in a high-speed blender and process until completely smooth. Transfer to a large mixing bowl.

To make the meringue mix, put the aquafaba in a separate bowl and beat with an electric whisk until it forms soft peaks. Add the sugar a spoonful at a time, whisking constantly, until it is all incorporated and the mix is thick and glossy.

Add a third of the meringue mix to the pistachio mix and mix gently to loosen it, then add another third of the meringue mix and fold it into the mix gently. Add the remaining meringue and carefully fold it through the mix. Scatter the remaining pistachios in a few at a time and gently stir them through until fully incorporated. Pour the mix into the lined loaf tin (pan) and put into the freezer for at least 6 hours or until frozen through.

Prepare the poached pears. Peel the pears, cut in half lengthways, scoop out the core and cut out the woody base, leaving the stalk intact for effect. Put the rest of the poached pear ingredients into a saucepan and add the pears. Gently bring to the boil and cover with a cartouche (see page 182). Simmer until the pears are just soft (but not breaking up). Remove from the heat and leave to cool in the liquid. Strain, then place in the fridge.

Place two pear halves on each plate and serve with a slice of the pistachio semifreddo.

I like my apple cake to be very moist and sticky, oozing caramelized sugars and apple juices everywhere. I grant you this is not very sophisticated, but it is very nice to eat. This is a lovely, gooey apple cake which is just perfect served with a generous dollop of ice cream.

Serves: 4

MOIST APPLE CAKE

with cashew ice cream

FOR THE CASHEW BASE (YOU WILL NEED TO PREPARE THIS 12–24 HOURS IN ADVANCE)
150g (5½oz/scant 1 cup) cashew nuts
150ml (5fl oz/⅔ cup) water
2 probiotic capsules

FOR THE ICE CREAM
250ml (8½fl oz/1 cup) water
250g (9oz/1¼ cups) caster (superfine) sugar
1g (scant ¼ tsp) sea salt
25g (1oz) glucose syrup
250g (9oz) cashew base

FOR THE SPONGE
180g (6½oz/1½ cups) plain (all-purpose) flour
4g (scant 1 tsp) bicarbonate of soda (baking soda)
5g (⅛oz/2 tsp) ground cinnamon
1g (scant ¼ tsp) sea salt
150g (5½oz/generous ¾ cup) soft brown sugar
110ml (3½fl oz/scant ½ cup) extra virgin olive oil
55ml (2fl oz/¼ cup) water
15ml (1 tbsp) cider vinegar
4 large Bramley apples, peeled, cored and cut into 1cm (½-inch) dice
50g (1¾oz/¼ cup) demerara sugar

First make the cashew base as it will need to be stored for 12–24 hours before it is ready to use. Blend the cashew nuts, water and the contents of the probiotic capsules together in a high-speed blender to a smooth paste. Leave in a sealed sterile container somewhere around 22°C (71°F) for 12–24 hours. It is ready when the mix has become foamy and smells sweet and cheesy. Once made, store in the fridge until needed.

To make the ice cream, heat the water, sugar, salt and glucose gently together in a small saucepan until the sugar dissolves.

Weigh the sugar syrup into a heatproof jug and make up to 525g (18½oz) with water. Add the cashew base and blend in a high-speed blender until very smooth. Process following the instructions on your ice-cream machine.

Next make the cake. Preheat the oven to (fan) 140°C/160°C/310°F/gas mark 2½. Grease and line a 20cm (8-inch) square, loose-bottomed baking tin (pan).

Mix the flour, bicarbonate of soda (baking soda), cinnamon, salt and brown sugar together in a large bowl. In a jug, mix the olive oil, water and cider vinegar together, then pour it into the flour mix. Using a spoon, mix gently until just combined – don't beat. Fold the diced apple in until well combined. Pour the mix into the prepared baking tin (pan) and level out. Sprinkle with the demerara sugar and bake for 30–40 minutes until the top is golden and it is cooked through (check by inserting a cocktail stick into the centre – it should come out clean). Leave to cool for 10 minutes, then remove from the tin (pan) and leave on a cooling rack until cold.

When ready to serve, slice the apple sponge. Place a slice of cake on each of 4 dessert plates and add a scoop of the cashew ice cream.

ICE CREAM VARIATIONS

Vanilla: Scrape in the seeds from 3 juicy vanilla pods before blending.
Nutmeg: Grate in ⅓ of a nutmeg before blending.
Cardamom: Add 20 crushed pods of green cardamom to the water and sugar before bringing to the boil. Leave for 5 minutes before straining and weighing the sugar syrup.

BREADS

A good rye bread is an essential recipe to have in your repertoire. The base of this recipe is a sour dough, which may make you worry it's going to be complicated, but the truth is it's the opposite. You have to give a little more forethought, thinking in days not hours, but sourdoughs are gentle creatures and can be easily sped up or slowed down with temperature changes.

Making the initial sour dough mix does take a while (five days to be exact), but it also takes just a minute or two a day; and once you have your "mother" you can just keep it rolling over, time after time.

Makes: 1 loaf

RYE BREAD

FOR THE RYE BREAD STARTER
| Day 1 |
50g (1¾oz/scant ½ cup) wholemeal (wholewheat) rye flour
100ml (3½fl oz/scant ½ cup) warm water (40°C/104°F)

| Days 2, 3 and 4 |
25g (1oz/scant ¼ cup) wholemeal (wholewheat) rye flour
50ml (2fl oz/scant ¼ cup) warm water (40°C/104°F)

| For the "mother" |
50g (1¾oz) rye bread starter (or reserved "mother")
175g (6¼oz/1½ cups) wholemeal (wholewheat) rye flour
350ml (12fl oz/1½ cups) warm water (40°C/104°F)

FOR THE RYE BREAD
450g (1lb) of "the mother" (see above)
345g (12oz/scant 3 cups) wholemeal (wholewheat) rye flour
3g (1½ tsp) caraway seeds (optional)
8g (¼oz/1½ tsp) sea salt
200ml (7fl oz/generous ¾ cup) water

On Day 1, mix the rye flour and water together in a small very clean container or jar and loosely place a lid on it (so air can get in). Leave in a warm place (around 22°C/71°F).

On Days 2, 3 and 4, add the rye flour and water to the mix each day, return the lid and place back in the warm place.

On Day 5 your mix should be bubbly and smell sweetly sour. It may have fermented, in which case it will appear separated with a liquid layer, but as long as it smells sweet and/or sour it will be ok. If it is mouldy or smells unpleasant then you'll have to throw it away and start again. If it isn't bubbling or smells like flour then it wasn't kept in a warm enough place – discard three-quarters of the mix and carry on adding flour and water for a few more days making sure it is kept in a warm enough place.

When the mix is ready you can create your yeast culture, the "mother". Mix all the "mother" ingredients together in a bowl. Cover with a tea towel and put somewhere warm for about 12 hours.

Now you can make the rye bread. Line a 900g (2lb) loaf tin (pan) with baking parchment. Weigh 450g (1lb) of the "mother" into a large bowl and keep the rest to refresh the "mother" (see box, below). Add the rest of the ingredients and stir to form a clay-like mix. Spoon into the prepared loaf tin (pan) – it should fill two-thirds of it – and smooth the top. Cover with cling film (plastic wrap) and put somewhere warm for 4–5 hours until risen to the top of the loaf tin (pan).

Preheat the oven to (fan) 170°C/190°C/375°F/gas mark 5. Remove the cling film (plastic wrap) and bake the bread for 45 minutes to 1 hour. When you think it's ready, remove from the tin (pan) and tap the bottom of the loaf, it should give a dull hollow thud. If it doesn't, bake for 20 more minutes. Allow to cool for 4 hours before cutting.

> **THE "MOTHER"**
>
> *The remaining "mother" can either have flour and water added to make bread again the next day, or you can put it in an airtight container in the fridge where it will keep for up to 1 month until you next want to make bread.*

Sometimes it is good to have a cracker that has a bit of character of its own. So often a cracker is just a vehicle to get whatever you've spread on it into your mouth, but not in this case. These traditional Scandinavian crackers are best paired with quite neutral pâtés and dips, anything too strong and the flavours may compete. If you want something with a little less character then simply omit the caraway seeds.

Makes 20 crisp breads

RYE CRISP BREADS

65g (2oz/½ cup) dark rye flour, plus extra to dust
65g (2oz/½ cup) wholemeal (wholewheat) spelt flour (or plain wholemeal/wholewheat flour)
10g (¼oz/1 tbsp) flax seeds
10g (¼oz/1¼ tbsp) sesame seeds
2g (1 tsp) caraway seeds
3g (½ tsp) sea salt
3g (¾ tsp) dried yeast
90ml (3¼fl oz/generous ⅓ cup) warm water (40°C/104°F)

Put all the ingredients in a bowl and bring together into a rough dough. Transfer to a clean work surface and knead for 5 minutes until the dough is smooth. Put back into the bowl and cover with cling film (plastic wrap). Place in a cool place (20°C/68°F) for at least 2 hours, but ideally 12–24 hours (the longer you leave it, the better it will taste).

Preheat the oven to (fan) 160°C/180°C/350°F/gas mark 4.

Dust your work surface with rye flour and divide the dough into 4. Roll each batch out as thin as you can – the thinner you roll it, the crisper the bread will be.

Cut the mix into your desired shape. I either make random shards approximately 5cm (2 inches) long or use a cookie cutter to get a neat round circular shape.

Line a baking tray (sheet) with non-stick baking parchment and arrange the crisp breads neatly on it, shaking as much flour from them as you can. Bake until golden and crisp – this will take up to 10 minutes, depending on how thin you rolled them.

Remove from the oven and allow to cool. These will keep for up to 4 weeks in an airtight container.

This Sardinian bread is supposed to be so thin before it's baked that you can read your music through it. I find it a great, crispy cracker to spread creamy pâtés on. Once made, the carta di musica will last a long time, provided they are kept dry, and are a handy bread to have to hand should you need an emergency cracker. I like to roll the dough through a pasta machine to ensure an even, ultra-thin end result, but you can roll it out by hand using a more traditional rolling pin and floured surface should you wish.

Serves: 8–12

CARTA DI MUSICA

100g (3½oz/scant ¾ cup)
    type 00 flour
90g (3oz/½ cup) fine semolina,
    plus extra to dust
2g (½ tsp) dried yeast
2g (⅓ tsp) sea salt
100ml (3½fl oz/scant ½ cup) water
extra virgin olive oil
coarse grain salt

Place the flour, semolina, dried yeast and sea salt in a bowl and add the water. Knead for about 2 minutes to make a smooth dough, then leave to rest in a warm place (about 22°C/71°F) for 1 hour to rise. Knock it back by kneading and punching the air out, then turn it out onto a work surface. Knead for 5 more minutes to achieve a supple elastic dough. Leave somewhere warm for 45 minutes to rise.

Preheat the oven to (fan) 160°C/180°C/350°F/gas mark 4.

If using a pasta machine, knock the dough back and cut it in half. Using the pasta machine, process half the dough at a time, as for pasta (see page 124), working down through the settings until it has gone through the second to last setting.

If using a rolling pin, knock it back and cut it into 6 balls. Roll out 1 ball as thinly as you can without the dough breaking.

Spread your rolled dough out on a clean work surface lightly dusted with semolina. Using a sharp knife cut the mix into 3cm (1¼-inch) strips along its width. Lay these strips out on a large baking tray (sheet) and bake in the oven for 5 minutes. You want them to puff up and cook but not go crispy. Remove from the oven and lay them out on your work surface.

Using a large flat surface, like a chopping board, squash the breads flat, applying a fair bit of pressure. Brush each bread lightly with olive oil using a pastry brush, and sprinkle a little coarse salt on top. Put the breads back onto the baking tray (sheet) and return to the oven for 5 more minutes until golden brown and crisp. Repeat with the rest of the mix.

When cool, these can be kept in an airtight container for up to 4 weeks.

This is a very quick bread to make and a great accompaniment to a wide variety of dishes. If you want to add another level of interest, sprinkle the breads with pistachio dukkah (see page 113), chilli flakes (crushed chillies) or herbs just after you drizzle them with olive oil.

Makes: 6

FLAT BREADS

335g (11½oz/2⅓ cups) type 00 flour (or strong white bread flour), plus extra to dust
7g (¼oz/1¼ tsp) sea salt
7g (¼oz/1¾ tsp) dried yeast
30ml (1fl oz/2 tbsp) extra virgin olive oil, plus extra to drizzle
215ml (7½fl oz/scant 1 cup) water

Place the flour, salt and yeast in a large bowl. Place the olive oil and water in a jug and mix with a fork, then pour into the dry ingredients. Mix with a dough scraper or spoon to form a rough dough, then turn out onto a clean work surface.

Knead the dough for about 8 minutes until soft and supple, then return to the bowl and cover with cling film (plastic wrap). Leave to prove somewhere warm for about 1 hour until it has doubled in size. Turn the dough out onto the work surface and knead for 2 minutes. Form into a ball and cut in half, then cut each half into thirds and dust lightly with flour.

Push each piece flat onto the work surface to form a disc and then fold one edge into the middle. Press it down with your thumb to stick, and turn the disc round a few centimetres (an inch). Bring the edge into the middle again and stick again. You will see a gluten layer stretching across the dough. Keep lifting, sticking and turning, going round 2 or 3 times, until the dough resembles a firm ball. Repeat for all the pieces and leave to rest, crease side down, for 15 minutes covered with a clean tea towel.

Lightly dust the work surface with flour and place one ball on it with the creased side down. Flatten with the palm of your hand, then, with a rolling pin, roll the dough to a circle 20–25cm (8–10 inches) wide. Using your fingers, stretch out the edges of the bread to thicken them slightly (like you would for pizza dough). Dust the dough with flour and set aside. Repeat for each ball of dough and leave for 20 minutes to rest.

Heat a large, heavy-based griddle pan until very hot (but not burning hot). Turn the temperature down to medium. Add one of the flat breads and cook until the underside is golden and the top has bubbled and puffed up. Flip the bread over and cook the other side for 2 minutes. Remove to a plate, bubbly side up, and drizzle lightly with olive oil and any other herbs you wish (see introduction, above). Repeat for each flat bread. Serve warm.

There are a lot of good bakers out there and a lot of seriously good books on making the perfect sourdough, artisanal loaf. Sourdough is a complex art and deserves more than a footnote in a book on other matters. What this is, however, is a way to bake a loaf that doesn't take five days and constant love and attention. You can either finish it on the day or leave the dough overnight in the fridge to develop a more complex flavour, without causing you too much bother.

Makes: 1 loaf

EVERYDAY BREAD

375g (9¾oz) warm water
5g (⅛oz/scant 1½ tsp) dried yeast
15g (½oz/2¾ tsp) fine sea salt
400g (14oz/2½ cups) strong white bread flour, plus extra for dusting
100g (3½oz/scant 1 cup) wholemeal bread flour

Mix the water and dried yeast together in a bowl and leave to dissolve for 10 minutes. Add the salt and both flours and mix into a rough dough, then cover with a large plate or cling film (plastic wrap) and leave for 15 minutes to rest.

After 15 minutes wet your hands and, grabbing the dough furthest away from you, lift it into the air and fold it down towards you so it comes over the top of the remaining dough, trying to visualise catching as much air as possible beneath. Turn the bowl by a quarter turn and repeat until you've done four lift and folds. Do another four turns and then cover again and leave for another 15–30 minutes. Repeat the lifting and folding routine process one more time and then turn the dough over so it's smooth side up.

Cover with a plate or cling film (plastic wrap). If you are baking the same day, leave the dough for 1 hour somewhere warm to prove and then bake as below. If you are baking the next morning, pop it in the fridge and leave it to prove overnight.

Put your casserole dish or Dutch oven in the oven to preheat to (fan) 200°C/220°C/425°F/gas mark 7. When you are ready to bake, uncover your dough (it should have doubled in size) and carefully turn it out onto a lightly floured work surface, trying not to deflate it. Take one side of dough and fold it over in thirds, gently trying to stick it together while stretching then turn it over so the smooth side is on top. Carefully lift it and put it into a floured proving basket. Dust with flour and leave for about 20 minutes until risen, but not too soft and puffy.

When the dough is risen, carefully remove the casserole from the oven. Gently tip the dough in and cut a large, deep score along the top. If you have them, put a couple of ice cubes in the bottom, put the lid on and put back in the oven.

Bake for 40 minutes then remove from the oven. Carefully remove the loaf from the casserole and, if it still isn't fully darkened, put it back in the oven until it reaches your desired colour. Remove from the oven and cool on a cooling rack until needed.

This is probably the most reliable bread recipe you can make at home. It's handy because it's one of the tastiest, too. If the method descriptions aren't obvious then I would recommend looking up a video online for any of the techniques included here.

Makes: 1 loaf

FOCACCIA

420ml (14fl oz/1¾ cups) warm water

4g (¾ tsp) dried yeast (8g/1½ tsp fresh)

12g (¾ tbsp) fine sea salt

500g (1lb 2oz/3½ cups) type 00 flour (or strong white bread flour)

50ml (2fl oz/scant ¼ cup) extra virgin olive oil

20g (¾oz) coarse salt (such as Maldon)

Put the warm water in a large mixing bowl and add the yeast. Leave the yeast to dissolve and disperse for 5 minutes.

Add the fine salt and 00 flour to the water and yeast mixture and stir to bring together into a smooth dough. Put in the bowl and cover with a large plate or cling film (plastic wrap) and leave for 15 minutes to rest.

After 15 minutes wet your hands and, grabbing the dough furthest away from you, lift it into the air and fold it down towards you so it comes over the top of the remaining dough, trying to visualise catching as much air as possible beneath. Turn the bowl by a quarter turn and repeat until you've done four lift and folds. Do another four turns and then cover again and leave for another 15–30 minutes.

Repeat the lifting and folding routine process one more time and then turn the dough over so it's smooth side up. Drizzle with a little of the olive oil and rub to coat. Cover with a plate or cling film (plastic wrap). If you are baking the same day, then leave it for 1 hour somewhere warm to prove then go to the next step. If you are baking the following morning, pop it in the fridge and leave it to prove overnight.

When you are ready to bake, remove the cover from your dough – it should have doubled in size. Take a large baking tin (tray) and line it with non-stick baking paper. Add a generous drizzle (2–3 tablespoons) of the olive oil and rub it with your hands to cover the base and sides of the lined tin. Without washing your hands (to make sure they are nicely oiled), lift the dough out of the bowl, trying to keep as much air in it as possible, and put it in the baking tin. Carefully fold one end over and then the other, imagining rough thirds, then place it in the middle of the tin. Tease it out slightly toward the edges and leave it to rest for about 1 hour.

Preheat the oven to (fan) 200°C/220°C/425°F/gas mark 7.

After an hour the dough should be bubbly and have spread out to the edges of the tin. If any parts haven't spread fully, just gently lift them and pull them out. Drizzle another generous amount of olive oil over the top then spread it out with your hands.

Spreading the fingers out on both hands, push down into the dough to the bottom, working over the whole dough to accentuate the bubbles. Sprinkle with the coarse salt and bake into the middle of the oven for 25–35 minutes until golden brown and crispy. Remove from the oven and leave to cool on a cooling rack.

| OILS, BUTTERS AND MILKS |

FENUGREEK OIL

Using this oil is a great way to add a subtle depth and interest to a dish without dominating it. This goes especially well with garlic and onion flavours and is a surprising partner for truffle.

Makes: 150ml (5fl oz/⅔ cup)

10g (¼oz/scant 1 tbsp) fenugreek seeds
150ml (5fl oz/⅔ cup) rapeseed oil

Put the fenugreek seeds and oil in a small saucepan and heat gently to 80°C/176°F. Remove from the heat, allow to cool, then transfer to a sealed bottle. Store for at least 2 weeks before using.

This will keep in the fridge for 3 months.

THYME OIL

This is a great way to add a little herbaceous interest to a dish without overwhelming it with greenery. It is also good to dip bread into, should the fancy take you.

Makes: 125ml (4fl oz/½ cup)

10g (¼oz) sprigs of thyme
1 small shallot, sliced
1 clove of garlic, peeled
1 dried red chilli
1 bay leaf, torn
5 peppercorns
125ml (4fl oz/½ cup) extra virgin olive oil

Put all the ingredients into a small saucepan. Very gently heat until the shallots begin to bubble. Remove from the heat and leave to cool.

Transfer to a jar and push down the solid ingredients so they are covered by oil. Leave for at least 8 hours, and ideally up to 2 weeks, to infuse. After 14 days strain the oil and discard the solids.

This will keep in the fridge for 3 months.

GARLIC PARSLEY OIL

This is an immensely useful thing to have in the fridge. Whenever you want to add a bit of depth to a dish just sprinkle this in, cook for a few minutes, and it will make it instantly delicious.

Makes: 200ml (7fl oz/generous ¾ cup)

10 cloves of garlic, peeled
15g (½oz/4 tbsp) parsley leaves, roughly chopped
175ml (6fl oz/¾ cup) extra virgin olive oil

Put all the ingredients into a blender and process until smooth.

This will keep in an airtight container in the fridge for up to 1 month.

LAVENDER OIL

You have to be a little careful with lavender. Just the right amount brings a subtle sophistication to a dish, but even a touch too much and it will make it taste like medicine. You want this oil to be obviously lavender flavoured but not bitter or overwhelming.

Makes: 125ml (4fl oz/½ cup)

10g (¼oz) sprigs of thyme
3g (4 tsp) dried lavender
125ml (4fl oz/½ cup) rapeseed oil

Put all the ingredients into a small saucepan and heat gently until the thyme just begins to bubble. Remove from the heat and leave to infuse for 4 hours. Taste, and if the lavender is pronounced but not overwhelming, strain. If not ready, leave a little longer and re-test, then strain.

This will keep in the fridge for 3 months.

PINE NUT BUTTER

This recipe is essential to producing elegant, artisan, plant-based food in the Italian tradition. The creamy moreishness of pine nuts combined with the buttery overtones of olive oil give this fridge staple essential status. If you are making it just for one recipe then simply make one batch, but I always multiply this recipe by at least four to have some to hand.

Makes: 175g (6¼oz)

100g (3½oz/¾ cup) pine nuts
25ml (1fl oz/5 tsp) Italian extra virgin olive oil
    (preferably Sicilian)
75ml (2¾fl oz/⅓ cup) water

Preheat the oven to (fan) 160°C/180°C/350°F/gas mark 4.

Put the pine nuts on a small baking tray (sheet) and roast in the oven for no more than 3 minutes – you are warming them, not colouring them.

Put the pine nuts, olive oil and water into a blender and blend until silky smooth. Pass through a sieve and store in a container.

This will keep in the fridge for up to 7 days.

HAZELNUT BUTTER

This butter brings both nuttiness and a luxurious richness to a recipe.

Makes: 220g (8oz)

110g (3¾oz/¾ cup) blanched hazelnuts
30ml (1fl oz/2 tbsp) hazelnut oil
85ml (2¾fl oz/⅓ cup) water
2.5g (scant ½ tsp) sea salt
2.5g (generous ½ tsp) caster (superfine) sugar

Preheat the oven to (fan) 160°C/180°C/350°F/gas mark 4.

Put the hazelnuts onto a small baking tray (sheet) and roast in the oven for 7 minutes until golden.

Put the roasted hazelnuts and the rest of the ingredients into a blender and blend until very smooth. This will keep in the fridge for up to 3 days.

ALMOND MILK

This recipe contains nothing but almonds, so all the body and flavour comes from the almond mass alone. Although this makes a thick milk, you can add up to double the water for a lighter version.

Makes: 250ml (8½fl oz/1 cup)

100g (3½oz/scant ¾ cup) whole almonds
300ml (10fl oz/1¼ cups) cold water

Put the almonds into a small bowl, cover with cold water by at least 2.5cm (1 inch), and put into the fridge overnight. When ready to make the milk, drain the almonds and rinse well. Transfer the almonds to a blender and add the measured water. Process for 1–2 minutes until smooth and creamy.

Line a sieve with a 45cm (18-inch) square piece of sterile muslin (cheesecloth) and set over a jug. Pour the mix into the muslin (cheesecloth) and collect up the corners to make a bag. Squeeze the bag to extract the milk into the jug until you are struggling to get much liquid.

The almond milk will keep in the fridge for up to 3 days.

SMOKED HAZELNUT MILK

This simple variation on nut milk adds a savoury depth wherever it is used, either as the base for a sauce or the sauce itself.

Makes: 200ml (7fl oz/generous ¾ cup)

80g (2¾oz/scant ⅔ cup) hazelnuts
200ml (7fl oz/generous ¾ cup) water
10ml (2 tsp) hazelnut oil
sea salt

Put 1 tbsp of hickory chips into a stove-top smoker. Line the top grate with foil to prevent the nuts from escaping, and follow the manufacturer's instructions. Smoke the nuts until they have a light smoky flavour.

Transfer the nuts to a blender with the water and oil and blend to a paste. Follow the method for almond milk (see above) to strain the milk through a muslin (cheesecloth), then season to taste. It should be rich, nutty and smoky. This will keep in the fridge for up to 3 days.

INDEX

ACKNOWLEDGEMENTS

Helen – I am only one half of everything we achieve, you have always been there, you cared for our family, tidied in my wake, ran the errands, picked up the pieces and kept me going whenever I wanted to stop. Nothing could have happened without you.

My parents – For always supporting me, for always being there and for always believing, even when you probably thought you shouldn't.

Rachel and Keith – For always being there when we needed you, for going above and beyond every day to help, just so I can make some vegetables hot.

Jo Edwards Castle Farm Organics – We have worked together for ten years now and without your perfectly wonky vegetables I could never have produced the food I have. Thank you for inviting us onto your farm for the photo shoot, rushing around finding "two leaves of this" and "another one of that but muddier", for helping to clean, providing tea and keeping me going. This book is as much about your farm as my food.

Over the years I have worked with too many amazing people to mention, needless to say I learnt something from every one of them and there is a piece of them all on every page of this book.

To the current chefs in the restaurant: Steve, Jamie, Jake, Jerome and Alfie – Thank you for not shouting when I stole your prep, pinched your deliveries and dumped my washing-up after a long day. Your skill and dedication never fails to inspire me.

Kev – Thank you for quietly keeping it all going and making it better.

Suresh – For having the patience to convince me this was a good idea and gently steering the ship.

Fritha – For seeing something and for gently and politely keeping everything on the straight and narrow.

A book is only partly about the recipes and the writing. Kim, your photographs make this book what it is. Tania, you have worked with endless changes in brief, edits and reshuffles and didn't swear at me once. Claire, for helping to turn what I think is right into what is better. Caroline, for endlessly wandering the south-west to find just the perfect plate. Silvana, for lending us your beautiful things at a moment's notice and never once complaining.

With thanks for the loan of ceramics to Elvis Robertson Ceramics, elvisrobertson.com, pages 21, 22, 49, 69, 81, 143, 146, 150, 171; residentstove.co.uk, page 84.

AUTHOR BIOGRAPHY

Richard was born and raised a vegetarian and studied literature and philosophy before moving into cooking.

In 2013, he opened Acorn Restaurant in Bath which subsequently became the first vegan restaurant in the UK to be listed in the Michelin Guide. Between lockdowns in 2020, Richard evolved Acorn into OAK to place a greater focus on sustainability in restaurants. OAK has held a Michelin Green Star since 2022.

Richard lives in Somerset in the UK with his family.